TAROT FOR SELF-REFLECTION:

A GUIDE TO JOURNALING WITH THE TAROT TO DEEPEN YOUR RELATIONSHIP TO YOURSELF AND YOUR CARDS

AMANDA KAY OAKS

ISBN 979-8-3303-2031-8

CONTENTS

Introduction
What is Tarot?

What is *Tarot*? Well, the short answer is it's an illustrated deck of roughly 78 cards, often used for divination and self-reflection. But really, if you ask ten witches what Tarot is, you'll probably get ten variations on the answer. Like so many magical tools, one's relationship to the cards and how to use them varies depending on the person and what they're seeking.

I've seen Tarot readers shrouded in mystery at the Renaissance Faire, promising to reveal your future. I've also had a Tarot reader sit at my kitchen table and read for my entire bachelorette party, to mixed results.

As for me? I was first drawn to Tarot as a socially anxious 20-something, looking for a way to give myself something to do at parties. It's interesting that I started teaching myself about Tarot to connect with other people, because these days, I spend most of my Tarot time alone, in quiet reflection with the cards.

So, to answer the question "What is Tarot?" from my personal lens? It's a deck of illustrated cards that are used to connect to your intuition; to learn more about yourself and what you might need to focus on right now. Contrary to popular belief, Tarot is not primarily a tool for predicting the future, telling you what's absolutely going to happen a week from now. It's more like a mirror, reflecting back what you're putting out.

Tarot decks are collections of archetypal images, associated with general meanings. Many modern decks loosely follow the style of the iconic Rider-Waite-Smith deck, though each deck brings its own imagery and ideas to the traditional meanings behind each card. This book will discuss the imagery and associations from the Rider-Waite-Smith deck, but you can certainly use and adapt the journal prompts for whichever deck you have in front of you. I recommend reading this book with your Tarot deck close to hand, as many of the journal prompts will ask you to reflect on the imagery of the cards in your specific deck.

In most decks, you will have two kinds of cards: the Major Arcana and the Minor Arcana. Major Arcana cards are numbered 0-22 and follow what's called the Fool's journey. It's the story of life, of adventure, and all of the ups and downs along the way. These are often considered bigger energy cards, suggesting you're tapping into something significant, or which is playing a big role for you right now.

The Minor Arcana consists of four suits, most often *Swords, Wands, Pentacles/Coins,* and *Cups.* Some decks will vary these suits with other names, but often maintain the same basic associations, which are as follows:

- Swords—Thoughts, the inner world
- Wands—Actions, creativity
- Pentacles/Coins—Stability, the physical world
- Cups—Emotions, feelings

Within the Minor Arcana, there are cards numbered 1-10, as well as "court cards" much like a deck of playing cards. The court cards are sometimes said to represent people and many Tarot guidebooks write about them as such. The numbered cards tell a story much like the Major Arcana but on a smaller scale, such as life's daily ups and downs, rather than its massive touchstone moments.

However, Tarot can be so much more than that. By sitting with your tarot cards regularly, you can begin to tap into your inner knowing and connect with what's sitting below the surface for you. If you always panic when you see The Tower or roll your eyes when the Page of Wands won't stop stalking you, that tells you something about where you're at and what you might need to work on. For instance, The Tower represents sudden, massive change. If it scares you, it's worth investigating why you're so resistant to change. Thinking through our relationship to the messages of cards in this way can help us unpack our thought patterns and habits and how they're serving us. Sure, The Tower can be scary, but sometimes, our lives *might* need to get a little shaken up.

This book is intended to help you develop a personal relationship with the Tarot and with your inner self. Think of it like meditations on the images and meanings of the cards, with the goal not to still your thoughts, but to know them intimately. I will not be teaching you how to predict the future or impress your friends at parties, but rather, we'll walk through the deck together to unpack what each card has to teach us about who we are, what we want, what we fear, and where we can expand and grow into who we want to be.

You can treat this book like a journey in chronological order if you like, journaling with each of the cards in the order they're presented here. Or, you could pull a card at random each morning and use the journal prompts to see what the card has to tell you for the day. There's no wrong way to journal with the Tarot, but it can be helpful to have some guidance when you're starting out. You can journal on every question I offer or pick one or two that resonate. This book is intended as a foundation to help you get started.

Let's find a quiet space, light some candles, and get to know ourselves and our Tarot cards.

CHAPTER 1

Picking a Tarot Deck

If you're new to Tarot or to journaling, you may be wondering how to get started. There's a myth that your first deck should be gifted to you, not purchased for yourself, but personally I think that's a bit of gatekeeping nonsense.

I bought my first Tarot deck in an occult shop in Glastonbury, where I was seized with the overwhelming sense that I just *had* to bring some of the magic home with me. My copy of *Tarot of the Cat People* was clearly used, the box scuffed and scraped, but all of the cards and the little guidebook inside were intact. I didn't know much of anything about Tarot back then, so I wasn't even aware there was an unspoken rule to break when I handed over a few pounds in exchange for this deck.

So, how do you pick a Tarot deck? For me, the most important thing is feeling a connection to the cards. Different decks use vastly different art styles, and you'll generally get more from a deck that resonates with you. If you don't like the art style of a particular deck, it's probably not the one for you, and that's okay. If you feel drawn toward a deck's theme or art style, however, that's a good sign that you'll enjoy working with it. For instance, as a college student who deeply missed her beloved cat back home, the cat person tarot spoke to me on a deeper level, and it was the deck I learned with for many years

Thus, my first bit of advice for picking a Tarot deck is to go somewhere where you can look at the art. Many stores will have opened copies of their decks that you can hold and browse through, but you can also opt to search for decks online and click through the images. Find art that speaks to you and makes you want to keep looking at it. So much of the language of Tarot is visual, which means you'll want to find a deck with imagery that speaks to you. A good Tarot deck will show you the story of the Fool's journey with the pictures on each card, so that you can begin to intuit the meaning of a card even before you crack open a book to look it up. When starting out, I suggest finding a deck with images that mean something to you.

That's not to say there is nothing else to consider, of course. If you are a beginner, I recommend making sure you've got a deck that's loosely modeled on the Rider-Waite-Smith style. How can you tell? You're looking for your standard deck of 78 cards, with the Major Arcana and four suits. Some decks use different names for the suits, but that's okay. Generally, a deck that has these components will be similar enough that most Tarot guides should work with what you've got. The little guidebook that comes with every Tarot book will help you navigate any differences in suit names or styles. You want to read this to better understand the author's vision for the deck.

One thing I would personally steer you against (for the purposes of using a Tarot deck for self-reflection and journaling) is what's known as a "pip" deck. These decks don't feature full illustrations for the Minor Arcana, opting instead for a simpler illustration with the number of Swords, Pentacles, etc. There's nothing wrong with this approach, of course, but it does mean you'll be missing the deeper images with layered meanings to reflect on.

In addition to the art style and format of the deck, something else to consider is the size and feel of the cards. It's not always possible to handle a deck before you buy, but online reviews and product descriptions will often give you some idea. Some decks are printed on various thicknesses of cardstock, with a glossy finish, while others may be matte. Some are larger than a deck of cards, while others may be more similar in size. You'll be spending a lot of time shuffling and handling your Tarot deck, so it's a good idea to make sure you find one that you can handle easily and feels good to you.

Picking Your Journaling Materials

Perhaps you picked up this book because you're an avid journaler, and you already know exactly what you like in a journal. That's great! Go forth with your favorite journal, pens, ink, and what you have. If you're not so sure, here are a few things you might consider. Some people who practice magic or work with Tarot prefer to have a separate journal/notebook for their Tarot practice. There are, in fact, plenty of journals specifically designed for recording daily Tarot card pulls, and you could certainly use one of those for the exercises in this book if you prefer.

However, a plain old journal works perfectly well. You can scribble in your Tarot journaling amongst whatever other journaling practices you may have, or you can dedicate a new notebook specifically to your Tarot journaling practice. The important thing is that you find a system that works for you. If you prefer lined paper because it keeps your handwriting neat, use a journal with lines. If you like to sketch alongside your journaling, go for a style that works for that purpose.

Much like picking a Tarot deck, the important thing in selecting a journal is making sure it's something that works for you. As a writer, many friends and family members have gifted me various journals over the years. I've found that some of them have cover textures that I don't like, or stiff pages that won't sit flat for me to write. Naturally, I don't like using these journals and they sit on the shelves untouched. Make sure you consider how it would feel to write in a notebook before you pick it for daily journaling practices, because you'll be much more likely to pick it up again if you have a pleasant experience.

The same goes for pens. Not everyone can spend delightful hours in the pen aisle, but that doesn't mean you won't discover some preferences when you're using your writing utensil on the daily. Some cheaper pens can become difficult to write with over time, while others with wet ink may smear easily. Test out some pens and use the one that makes writing feel effortless. You don't have to use the same writing utensil every time you journal, of course, but if you like a consistent look, make sure you keep track of it or have spares on hand.

I know what some of you might be thinking, but what if I prefer to journal digitally? I'll confess my bias here; I find journaling feels more magical when I do it with a good old pen and paper. I like to be screen-free while I sit and reflect on my Tarot card of the day, because it just works best for me. That doesn't mean you can't use a digital journal for this practice if it suits you—like I said, do what works.

Once you've picked out your Tarot deck and your journaling materials, we're ready to begin! This book is designed to guide you through getting to know your deck, but by all means, spend some time getting acquainted before you begin if you prefer. When you're ready, let's make some Tarot magic together!

Section One: The Major Arcana

The Major Arcana are the "big energy" cards of the Tarot. They're the ones you've most likely seen before if you're coming to Tarot through representation on TV and film. They are the most easy to recognize and have names that do some of the work for you, and they tend to get used in pop culture more frequently.

The Major Arcana cards are numbered 0-22 and, when laid out from beginning to end, tell a story known as the Fool's Journey. The figure from the first card, 0, is our Fool, and the cards 1-22 represent the different experiences that someone will go through in life, such as learning, change, falling in love, and reaching a state of completion. Each card has a name as well as a number, and these names often help us to understand what the card means, even before digging into the rich symbolism featured in the Tarot illustrations.

In our lives, we all experience the various parts of the Fool's Journey at different points, and we'll encounter them more than once. Therefore, even though they *can* tell a linear story, they typically don't and will pop into your readings whenever the moment is right for you to reflect on that aspect of the journey of life.

Because these cards represent the larger beats in the story of life, they are generally considered to be a stronger energy or influence when they come up in a reading. In other words, when you draw a lot of Major Arcana cards in a reading, it's time to pay attention and do some serious reflecting because you may well be in the midst of or getting ready to enter a pivotal point in your life's path.

CHAPTER 2

0: The Fool

The word "fool" has a bit of a negative connotation to it, which can make this card seem less than ideal to someone who's new to tarot. Who wants to be seen as a fool, after all? I prefer to think of The Fool as a beginner, inviting us to step into what one of my favorite yoga teachers calls the "beginner's mind." The story told by the Major Arcana is often called The Fool's Journey for a reason—we all start at the beginning and make our way through life, accumulating experiences and knowledge as we go. This card represents the start of a new journey.

In the Rider-Waite-Smith depiction, The Fool is a young person standing at the edge of a cliff. We can't see what lies ahead, and presumably neither can they. But they don't look worried about it in the least. Their posture suggests energy and excitement for whatever journey they're about to undertake. The Fool holds a stick with a small bundle tied around it in one hand. To me, this suggests that they are bringing some experience with them, but it isn't much—after all, that bundle couldn't hold the wisdom of some of our more experienced Tarot figures. In their other hand, The Fool lightly holds a fresh-picked rose. Like everything else in their attitude, this gesture appears carefree and easy. The flower is a beautiful thing, but The Fool isn't overly focused on protecting it or keeping it safe. It's there while it's there, and that's just fine.

The Fool isn't entirely alone here, either. At their feet is a small dog, who likewise looks energetic and ready to go. An eager companion who may not have too much to add in the way of experience or resources. Nevertheless, the dog is a reminder that we don't need to travel through life's new adventures entirely on our own. Sometimes a companion is a nice thing to have, even if they may not have much more knowledge about where we're going than we do.

In essence, The Fool is a card that shows up when we're at the start of something new, or when we need to look at life through a different perspective. You might see this card when you've accepted a new job offer or moved to a new city—there's a lot to learn, and even if you're bringing a ton of experience from other parts of your life, there's also a lot you can't yet know about your new situation. Remember the wisdom of the fool they're not afraid of the unknown, not yet. Rather, they're eager to see what's going to come next! Just make sure to prepare what you can in that little bundle of yours. You want to harness the energy of The Fool, but that doesn't mean you need to be foolish and walk into your new circumstances entirely unprepared.

If it truly feels like there's nothing new under the sun for you, The Fool can also be seen as an invitation to step into that beginner's mindset. Perhaps you've been feeling stagnant or restless and need to take a moment to imagine what your life would look like to The Fool version of you. Look back on how far you've come and remember how amazing so much of your day-to-day routine might seem to the self you were before you took that brave step over the cliff.

Journal Questions for The Fool

• These journal questions are great for when you're embarking on something new, whether you pulled The Fool in a reading or just want to reflect on that Fool energy as you enter a beginning phase of life. The New Moon is also a great time to reflect on this card, as it's the beginning of the next moon phase, just as The Fool begins the Major Arcana journey.

• Return to the images on this card (or reflect on it for the first time). Take the time to really look at what's pictured. What sticks out to you about The Fool? How do the images make you feel? Do they remind you of anything?

• When was the last time you tried something new? How did that experience go for you? Were you successful, or did you meet challenges along the way?

• What comes to mind when you think about being a beginner? Does this scare you, excite you... a mix of both? Take time to reflect on your relationship to the idea of new beginnings.

• Is there something new that's beginning, or about to begin, in your life? What can you do to prepare for this new opportunity or journey?

• As you prepare for a new journey, it's also important to consider what you've already got at your disposal. What do you already have that can benefit you as you set out? What do you hope to learn and add to your pack along the way?

CHAPTER 3

Honing Your Craft with
The Magician

I: The Magician

Whenever I pull The Magician, my first thought is, "You have everything you need to accomplish your goals." The figure in this card has gathered all his tools and laid them out before him. He looks like he is about to get some magic going.

In the Rider-Waite-Smith rendition, The Magician is wearing loose, flowing robes. His whole pose screams poise and balance. One hand is raised to the sky, the other pointing down to the ground, embodying the common phase "as above, so below." This is someone who is grounded and connected to the everyday, but is also open to the spiritual guidance from above. The infinity symbol floats above them, sealing in this idea of an unbroken flow between the realms.

Even the candle he holds is balanced, with a flame burning at both ends. Though I tend to think of The Magician as a relatively positive card, you can't help but feel a bit of warning in that depiction of a candle that's going to burn out quickly and burn the one who's holding it. It's a reminder that even though you may have everything you need to take the next steps, you don't have to do it all at once.

And speaking of the tools you need, they're all right here as well. On the table in front of him, The Magician has assembled representations of each suit in the Tarot. There's a pentacle, a cup, a wand, and a sword, all sitting at the ready to partake in the ritual he's about to perform. Since the suits also represent the elements, we have earth, water, fire, and air at the ready as well, the common ingredients in any magical ritual.

This is a table set and ready to make some magic, and pulling this card means that you're all set to make something. While it may be a fancy ritual involving flowing robes, most often, it's likely some other project you've been working towards for a while. It could be that next creative venture you keep daydreaming about but haven't started, or it might be a big project at work. Whatever you've been yearning to do, The Magician is a good indicator that all that thinking and dreaming likely means you've been laying the foundation to make it happen. So, why not pick up those tools and get to work?

Journal Questions for The Magician

• Take a moment to sit with your version of this card and reflect on its imagery. What sticks out to you about this card? How do the images make you feel? Do they remind you of anything?

• When you think of making the magic happen, what comes up for you? What goals, dreams, or projects seem magical to you at this moment?

• What are the tools you need to accomplish that thing you've been dreaming of doing? Take a moment to list what you *actually* need to get started versus the things you don't really need but tell yourself you do. How many of these tools do you already have at hand, and how many would be relatively easy to assemble?

• Consider the amount of balance in your own life. How connected are you to the mundane everyday realities of your life? Could you stand to take more notice of them? What about your spiritual side/higher self? The Magician is an invitation to bring a little of that "as above, so below" balance into your own life, so consider where this may be lacking for you.

• The Magician has everything they need at their disposal, making this card an invitation to consider what we already have. What are your skills and strengths? How are you already making the magic you want to see in your life?

CHAPTER 4

II: The High Priestess

Where The Magician is a reminder that you've assembled the tools you need for the task at hand, The High Priestess is all about connecting with the resources that are already within you. Seeing The High Priestess, for me, always feels like a breath of fresh air—and a bit of a friendly rebuke from the cards, as well. It's like they're saying, "Why are you asking *me* when you already know?"

The High Priestess is depicted seated on a throne, between two tall pillars. She sits erect, but relaxed—sure enough of her abilities and her position that she feels no need to put on airs. Her robes are long and flowy, making it hard not to associate The High Priestess with her witchy, magical leanings. She may be shrouded in mystery, but we get the sense she's perfectly content with who she is.

In her hands, she clutches a scroll, presumably full of wisdom or guidance. She and her notes are all she needs at this moment, a strong reminder that we are often our own best teacher and guide if only we learn to tap into our intuition (and maybe journal about it so we don't forget what we learn).

A crescent moon lies at her feet, another symbol speaking to the inner knowing that The High Priestess evokes. The moon is all about intuition and the unseen, as we'll discuss much later on in our journey through the Higher Arcana. Here, though, it feels less like a warning about the unseen and more like a talisman indicating that The High Priestess has tapped into her own hidden depths and brought them to submission—they are, after all, literally at her feet.

When The High Priestess comes up in a Tarot reading, it's often a hint that you already know the answer to your question, deep down. She's telling you to trust your inner wisdom and stop letting all the noise distract you from what you already *know*. Why do you think she keeps her throne room so empty? It's so she can better focus on what matters—that which lies within her.

Journal Questions for The High Priestess

• What comes to mind for you when looking at your deck's version of The High Priestess? What symbols or aspects of the card stick out? How does it make you feel?

• How often do you listen to your gut and your instincts? Think back over a time when you've had big decisions ahead. Did you have a sense of what you wanted to do deep down? If so, was it easy to follow that hunch, or did you experience doubt? If not, why do you think that is?

• Sit in quiet meditation for a few minutes, perhaps reflecting on your question or problem if you pulled this Tarot card to get some answers. Just notice what thoughts come to mind for a bit. Then, write them down. What did you learn about where you're at in relation to the issue or just at this moment in time? Practicing this exercise regularly can help you get more in tune with your inner High Priestess energy.

• What does "inner knowing" mean to you? Do you trust your own instincts, or do you tend to need more logic and research before coming to a decision? How might you unite the two, if you feel The High Priestess is inviting more intuitive thinking into your life?

• The High Priestess gives some major affirmation energy, so let's take a moment to tap into that sense of confidence. Set a timer for 1 minute and start complimenting yourself with reflections like "I am strong" and "I am capable." Whatever feels salient in this moment and whatever comes to mind, write it down. Bonus points if you read your positive comments aloud to yourself in the mirror.

CHAPTER 5

III: The Empress

The Empress is *Mother* energy, through and through. As depicted in the Rider-Waite-Smith variation, you get the sense she might well be pregnant as she sits on her cushy, comfy throne. Her breasts and stomach have a nice curve to them, one that dares you to deny her feminine energy and fertility.

That so-called throne she's sitting on looks more like a cozy armchair or a pile of pillows, really. She's got a blanket, and her dress is loose and flowy. Everything about her screams comfort and softness; all those traditionally feminine qualities, really. In her raised hand, she holds a scepter that brings to mind, well, a baby's rattle, another symbol that points to the idea that The Empress is undeniably a nurturing mother at her core.

In case we manage to miss the point, the card has another clue to really hone in on the whole feminine energy: a heart with the symbol for female rests at the bottom of her cozy cushions.

The Empress, then, is an invitation and reminder to connect with our feminine energy. Yes, men and nonbinary friends, you can connect to your feminine energy, too. If you—like me—aren't the mothering sort, that doesn't mean The Empress doesn't have a valuable message for you. The feminine connects to many things, including compassion, emotional awareness, and giving birth to *creative* pursuits, as well as, yes, occasionally to human beings. When this card comes up, chances are you're missing something where these traditionally feminine energies are concerned. Maybe you've been feeling less than fertile creatively, or perhaps you've been pushing through task after task without pausing to connect with how you *feel*.

Yeah, this whole book is about journaling with the tarot, but I think Mother Empress is a card that begs you to draw a hot bath or snuggle into some warm blankets, and journal about your feelings to make sure you're not ignoring them.

Journal Questions for The Empress

• Take a few moments to study The Empress card. What do you notice? What stands out for you, and why do you think you are particularly drawn to those aspects of the image?

• What does the word "feminine" mean to you? What is your relationship to the idea of femininity and its traditional depictions? How do you, or do you not, express femininity in your day-to-day life?

• What does "mother" mean to you? Are you a mother, or do you hope to become one? What is your relationship like with your own? If this question makes you uncomfortable, take some time to consider why that may be.

• Alternatively, or in addition, if you're the extra credit type, what does creation mean to you more broadly? What do you hope to give birth to or leave behind as your legacy in life?

• How does it feel to express or talk about your emotions? Do you find it easy to know how you feel, or do you lean more toward logic for your decision-making? How has this served you in the past?

CHAPTER 6

IV: The Emperor

The Emperor is, no doubt, the man in charge. When this card comes up, it's time to take control of the situation and honor your power.

The Emperor sits on a throne, and everything about him says "don't mess with me." He sits firmly upright, gripping a rod in one hand and an orb in the other, reminiscent of a king at his coronation. There's an ease to this posture, as if he's been sitting on this throne a long while and knows what he's doing. The nice long beard adds to the effect of seasoned wisdom and authority. Yet, lest we think he didn't earn his place, The Emperor appears to wear full plate armor beneath his kingly robes, a reminder of the battles it took to get him here. While he may sit easy on the throne now, it wasn't always that way, and he's not about to let you forget it. He's still got the protection around, just in case, because he knows where there's power, there is someone who's going to try and challenge it.

When I see The Emperor, I know I need to stop being so scared of hurting other people's feelings and stand firm in my convictions. It's a time for authority, for acknowledging when you know your stuff, and reminding others of what you bring to the table. This doesn't come naturally to me and can be difficult for many people raised as women, but it's an important skill to cultivate.

The Emperor can also represent existing structures and establishments, which means there's definitely room to see this guy as a stand in for the Patriarchy or for a Father Figure. If this card comes up when you're butting up against some frustrations with the systems that be, well, it can represent those systems as much as it affirms your need to fight against them as best you can. Likewise, if you're dealing with daddy issues, this card might pop up to remind you that your relationship with your father or father figure is something you need to address at this point in your life.

Journal Questions for The Emperor

• When you look at The Emperor, what do the images evoke for you? What stands out, and why do you think that might be?

• Where are the places in your life where you hold power or authority? This might be in a traditional sense, like being a supervisor or teacher, or it may be the power that comes from knowledge and experience. How do you show up in these areas where you are—or could be—the boss?

• What is your relationship to authority, both your own and that of others? Is it easy for you to take charge, or do you prefer to let others lead?

• Is there an issue or area of your life where you could stand to be a bit firmer? Take some time to consider ways that you can embrace or cultivate power in those areas of your life where you might sometimes let your own needs take a back seat.

• Alternatively, maybe you show up with your power turned up too high and need to consider how you might let others speak up from time to time. Consider where in life you might take up more space than is necessary, and how you might make room for others to share their ideas and values.

CHAPTER 7

V: The Hierophant

There is arguably no card in the Tarot with which I have a more complicated relationship with than The Hierophant. You see, you can use numerology to calculate your Tarot birth card, using the numbers from your date of birth. When I came across this information online, I immediately had to know which of the Major Arcana was my guiding light… and I was immensely disappointed when my birthdate led me to number 5, The Hierophant. Let me be clear here—there are no bad cards in Tarot, and this was entirely my own bias about the card that created these feelings. Investigating these kinds of reactions in ourselves can lead to a deeper understanding of how we interact with the world, which is why I share them with you here.

The Hierophant is all about rules and structure, about keeping with the status quo and doing things as they've always been done. He is an authority figure, sometimes a religious one or a teacher. And me? I wanted to see myself as a free spirit, as someone who would stand for what's right, not always with tradition. And yet... I have to admit, in my bones, I've always been a bit of a rule follower—the kind of girl who judges people for ignoring clearly printed signs in shops or for crossing the street outside of a crosswalk. So, yeah, I guess it makes since I was born under The Hierophant, even if I don't *want* it to. Over the years, though, I've learned that The Hierophant, like all cards, isn't bad. Tradition and structure can be important, after all, as long as we learn to identify when it's time to shake things up.

The Hierophant embodies that balance just as he sits in his clear position of authority. Rider-Waite-Smith depicts The Hierophant in robes on a throne, and it's clear from the crosses down the front that we're meant to see them as a religious leader. He has both hands raised, one holding a staff, and it isn't hard to imagine this figure laying down the law.

Clearly, he's got some things to say, and expect the two figures kneeling on either side of the card to take note. They are depicted as much smaller than The Hierophant, presumably bowing and deferent, awaiting instructions from their leader.

At The Hierophant's feet, there are two crossed keys. The duality here again reminds us of the importance of balancing our power, our history, and our adaptability. The keys themselves speak to unlocking knowledge, holding the answers to life's important questions. The Hierophant may be the owner of these keys, but they are not in his hands—they are waiting to be picked up by the followers to take this knowledge out into the world and bring about change.

When I see The Hierophant in a reading, it often takes a moment to parse through which version of this card is showing up. Sometimes, The Hierophant can be a message about stepping into a leadership role. Perhaps you've been considering teaching a class or taking on a management position. The Hierophant can be a signal that now is the time! Alternatively, the card might signal that *you* will be the student and that you're about to find a teacher with wisdom to impart. If you've been seeking a mentor or some guidance, this might be a sign to look around you and see if that person has already made themselves known to you.

On the flipside, I think The Hierophant can also be a reminder that some rules are meant to be broken. This card represents the rigidity that comes from blindly following tradition without questioning who it does—and doesn't—serve. Whenever I see this card, I take a moment to consider where I might be doing things out of habit without examining the bigger picture.

Journal Questions for The Hierophant

• Take a moment to look at and reflect on the imagery of The Hierophant. What images stick out to you? Why might that be?

• What is your relationship to tradition? What does this word evoke for you? Are there traditions that you need to re-examine or re-invigorate in your life?

• What is your relationship to authority? Do you like to be in charge or to be led? How has this served you in the past?

• What knowledge can you pass on to others? Where is there learning that you may still need to do? What steps can you take to exchange knowledge with others if this is something that is lacking in your life right now?

• Sometimes, The Hierophant points to someone in our lives we could stand to learn from. Can you identify people in your life who might be able to teach you something, even if they aren't in a traditional role of authority?

VI: The Lovers

Ah, The Lovers card. When I think about pop cultural representations of the Tarot, this is one of the cards that most often pops up in depictions of mysterious Tarot readings that predict the future. Indeed, looking at the card, The Lovers does, at first glance, seem very much like the image of a romantic partnership.

The Rider-Waite-Smith imagery for The Lovers looks like a union blessed by the angels—literally. An angel with his arms and wings spread wide takes up the top half of the card, seeming to bless and approve the meeting of our two nude lovers below.

The man and woman on the card are naked, and our female-coded figure stands beside a tree in which a serpent looks. It is, in other words, impossible to miss the Garden of Eden imagery going on here. The woman may as well be Eve, and she stands with her hand outstretched to Adam. The original lovers themselves, yearning to unite.

But it's hard to forget what else is lurking in the imagery here—things aren't going to stay perfect and idyllic for our lovers forever. The snake and the tree of knowledge are lying in wait, representing the challenges that life will throw in the paths of partnerships along the way. Eve has a decision to make—choose to follow God and Adam without question or see what the Snake is going on about with these apples on the tree of knowledge.

Basically, The Lovers is a card with a lot going on. One thing is certain—whether it refers to a romantic relationship, a friendship, a business union, or your relationship with yourself, The Lovers means that there's big relationship energy coming up for you right now. It's a time to examine the role of love in all its forms. What relationships are central to your life at this moment, and how are they serving you? When I was unhappily single, I used to hope this card meant I was about to meet a new romantic partner and fall madly in love. In my experience, though, it's much more likely that you're going to see The Lovers when an existing relationship or partnership in your life needs some kind of attention. More likely than not, the person who's standing in this energy with you right now is someone you already know. Heck, it might even be you.

If you've been questioning an existing relationship or wondering whether to enter into one, this card is a reminder that the time for making a decision is coming up. You have a choice to make, and it's time to weigh those options and move forward.

Journal Questions for The Lovers

• This card has a lot of symbolism and opportunities for messages to stick out to you. What parts of the image resonate for you right now? What are you drawn to, and why?

• What is your relationship to the idea of partnership? Do you have a romantic partner? Do you want one? Or are platonic relationships at the center of your world right now?

• If the Snake represents choices, what might this mean for you when it comes to your relationships right now? Are there particular relationships that seem due for some reflection? If so, spend some time considering where you may be at a decision point, and how to move forward.

• Let's think about that angel for a minute. They're giving their blessings to the union that's about to take place. What in your life would get that seal of approval from you right now? If the answer is nothing, what would it take for you to find something that you can welcome with your arms wide open?

• The Lovers can also represent partnerships in work and business. If you've been approached with an opportunity to partner up with someone new on a project or collaborate in a new way, this card may well be an invitation to consider how that partnership feels. Spend some time writing out the pros and cons of jumping into this business relationship, and remember, gut feelings count here, too.

CHAPTER 9

VII: The Chariot

When I think of The Chariot, it's all about forward momentum. That doesn't mean this card is about actual movement or travel (though it can be). Rather, The Chariot is a call to grab life by the reigns and take action.

The Chariot depicts a person standing firm at the helm of his chariot. He is fully outfitted in armor, showing that he is prepared for the situation he's charging towards here. The shoulder plates of the armor just so happen to look like crescent moons, lest we forget the importance of that internal, emotional preparation as well. The Chariot's driver knows their stuff inside and out, and he's ready to get going.

It's important to note that the driver doesn't hold reigns but rather clasps a single magic wand in their left hand. This may not be the best idea in real life, but in the Tarot, this signifies that the person has faith that he's headed in the right direction—he don't need to keep such a tight grip on his steeds to wind up where they want to go. It's not a physical connection that moves this vehicle forward, but sheer determination (and maybe a bit of magic). This isn't a card for uncertainty or deliberating—it's for taking charge.

The horses (or sphinxes, in this case) that lead the Chariot are opposites in both their colors and their directions. One leads left, the other leads right. Even so, the driver isn't worried about it. He has the confidence and the willpower to keep things in check and balance out these opposing forces to make things happen.

The Chariot may come up when you've reached a big decision and it's time to act on it. Maybe you've been meaning to leave that soul-sucking job or end that emotionally unbalanced relationship. You have the destination in mind, and you're just waiting for the will. This is the signal that you're ready, so get going.

Journal Questions for The Chariot

• Take a look at the symbolism of The Chariot. What sticks out to you in this image? Why do you think that is?

• Where could your life use a bit more forward momentum? Are you feeling stuck or stagnant somewhere, even if you know deep down how you'd like to change things?

• What would it mean to loosen up your grip on the reins of life just a bit? Where can you afford to let go and trust that the horses of your life will still go the right way in the end?

• Take a moment to reflect on any big changes or decisions that you feel called to make. Are you all suited up and ready to take action? If so, what's stopping you?

• Perhaps The Chariot suggests you've already been going full speed ahead for a while. If so, how is all that forward motion serving you? Is it maybe time to take a pause and take stock before your next big adventure?

CHAPTER 10
Honor Your Power with Strength

VIII: Strength

When I pull the Strength card, it always gives me a bit of an "oh shit" reaction, for some reason. It's not a negative card, or even one that comes with much of a warning, but for my people-pleasing personality, pulling Strength always feels a bit like I'm being chastised. Charging into any situation with confidence and bravery isn't exactly my go-to move, so this card often shows up for me when I've been avoiding something.

Make no mistake; the Strength card isn't your stereotypical muscle-bound, brute force kind of strength. No, we're talking about inner strength and courage with this one. Just one look at the artwork should make that clear, as it's really a fairly peaceful card.

A woman leans over a lion, giving it a gentle pat on the head. The normally fearsome creature, a symbol of power in its own right, has been tamed by this woman's calm demeanor. Her inner strength radiates from her calm, certain posture. She knows that she can trust the lion not to bite her, and she isn't afraid to get up close and person with it as a result.

Her dress is adorned with flowers, showing her certainty about the natural world and her place within it. Like the Magician, an Infinity symbol floats over her head, letting us know that Strength is tapped into the wisdom of the Universe. There's a balance here, as she's both grounded to the practical, present moment and open to the wider, mystical potential out there as well.

Strength is a reminder to harness your inner power and get on with it already. Perhaps you're hesitating about something, or you've been letting other people take advantage of you. It's long past time to stand up for yourself and be brave—but that doesn't mean plowing right through other people's feelings. Like the woman's calm approach to taming the lion, you should bring compassion with you when you fight your battles. But you *do* need to fight them.

Journal Questions for Strength

• When you look at this card, who do you relate to more—the woman or the lion? Are you in a position of power in your life right now, or are you allowing yourself to be tamed?

• What does the word "strength" mean to you? Do you feel like you are capable of embracing your inner strength, or does the very idea make you nervous? What past experiences have contributed to this relationship to the notion of strength?

• When you think about your own strengths, what comes to mind? Take a moment to remember where your strengths lie. Write down what you're good at, and don't be shy.

• Where in your life do you need to bring a little more courage? What have you been avoiding, or where have you allowed yourself to take a back seat when you want to be at the wheel? How can you move towards a place of bravery and strength in these aspects of your life?

• Who in your life embodies the Strength card? In other words, when you think of someone who is strong, who comes to mind? What can you learn from that person?

IX: The Hermit

In many ways, I see The Hermit as the patron saint of introverts. He is, as the name suggests, alone. The modern day version of this card is a Friday night spent curled up under the blankets with a good book (or a good show on Netflix).

In the Rider-Waite-Smith rendition, The Hermit is a wise old figure with a hooded cloak. He is shrouded in mystery, and he likes it that way—like any hermit, this figure keeps to himself. In his right hand, he grasps a gnarled walking stick. This tool is his support on the journey ahead, something he has perhaps created himself to aid him along the way so he needn't ask anyone for help. In his left hand, held aloft, is a brightly shining lantern. This light will guide him on his path, suggesting that The Hermit has the wisdom he needs to move forward.

And yet, for all this self-possession, The Hermit is hunched over a bit. Perhaps from age, yes, or maybe because none of us were really built to be alone *all* the time.

To me, The Hermit has a bit of a dual message for us. At its core, this card is an invitation to seek inward. It often comes up in our readings when we're in desperate need of some quiet, reflective time. Perhaps you're feeling called to stay in and read on Friday nights, or perhaps you're interested in learning about something new that will require time and dedicated study. Maybe you just need *one* night to yourself. Often, The Hermit is a call to take time to be alone so that you can listen to what your inner knowing has to say. There might be something, you know, deep down, but haven't taken the time to really hear yourself saying.

On the other hand, I sometimes see The Hermit as a warning. Do you want to be the old figure alone on a cliff, with only his own staff and lantern for company? If you don't take time to occasionally come out of your Netflix blanket nest and nurture your relationships, this is the fate that might await you. If you pull The Hermit and you know darn well that you've had plenty of "you-time" lately, he might be here to remind you that the time for Hermitting has passed, and you need to get out there again, at least for a little while.

Journal Questions for The Hermit

• Take a moment to look at the imagery on this card. Sparse though this particular illustration is, do you feel drawn to any of the elements of The Hermit's image? Why do you think that is?

• When was the last time you truly *listened* to yourself? Are you in tune with your inner voice, or do you tend to fill your days with other noise to block yourself out?

• What does truly restorative alone time look like for you? When you have time to yourself, what is the ideal way to spend it to recharge and refill your cup?

• How do you know when you've been in Hermit mode for too long? What signs suggest you may need to re-engage with other people, at least for a little while?

• If you're an extrovert who has the opposite problem, how do you know when it's been too long since you've taken a moment to be on your own?

CHAPTER 12

Embrace Impermanence with The
Wheel of Fortune

X: The Wheel of Fortune

You know the old saying "What goes up, must come down"? That's the Wheel of Fortune is, in a nutshell. Depending on where you're at in the wheel's rotation, this can be a welcome reminder or an anxiety-producing one. At its core, the Wheel of Fortune is a reminder about the inevitability of impermanence. Whether you're on top of the world or feel like you're bearing the weight of it, things are going to change eventually.

Imagery-wise, the Wheel of Fortune is a dense card. At its center, we have a wheel, of course. There's an inner and outer circle, each full of mysterious symbols that might tell you what was coming if only you could read them. These symbols do actually have meaning, but you have to hold a particular knowledge set to recognize them. On the outer wheel, we have the Hebrew letters YHVH (spelling out the name of God), and TORA (perhaps the Latin ROTA, meaning wheel). The symbols on the inner wheel are alchemical symbols, representing mercury, sulfur, water, and salt, once considered the building blocks of life. In essence, the Wheel of Fortune holds all the elements of physical life and the spiritual one.

Atop the wheel perches a sphinx, the mythical creature known to be fond of riddles and, therefore, representing knowledge and wisdom. Below lurks a demonic figure, flanked by a snake, both images that make us think of the underworld and the devil.

As if that wasn't enough, this card is also full of clouds that play home to four other winged figures, one a clear angel, while the others are various winged animals. They all hold books that they're carefully reading, as if studying the fates to predict what might happen next. Yup, this card is as busy as life itself, full of potential meaning to unpack.

In short, the Wheel of Fortune is... kind of a lot. This makes sense when we consider that the card is a representation of the circle of life itself—also (we hope) kind of a lot. This card comes as a reminder that life is full of cycles, that it has both its ups when we're sitting high on life and feeling like we've got it all under control, and its downs when we may as well be in the underworld since everything feels like it's on fire. When this card comes up during a hard time, it's a friendly reminder that things won't be this bad forever. And, if things are going pretty darn well, yeah, I don't like to see this card then. However, it does serve as a reminder that we should be grateful for and recognize the good times because, sadly, they won't last forever. Particularly not if we take them for granted.

Journal Questions for Wheel of Fortune

• You could probably write a whole dissertation on the imagery of this card alone, but I'm going to ask you to take a look again anyways. Which of this card's bountiful images draws your attention the most right now? Why might that be?

• Where are you on the wheel of life right now? Is this an "up" or a "down" period in the cycle? What makes you think that?

• Take a moment to reflect on what it feels like when you're at the top of the wheel. What does life look like for you then? How might you harness those feelings even when times are hard?

• Now, take some time to reflect on what it feels like when you're in a downswing. What helps you get through challenging times in your life?

• What does impermanence mean to you? When you think about the fact that life is a constant string of changes, how does that make you feel?

CHAPTER 13
Reap What You Sow with Justice

XI: Justice

The word "justice" always makes me think of the legal system, but this card doesn't (always) mean there's a legal case at hand. Justice, as the scales she holds implies, gives off big "for every action, an equal and opposite reaction" vibes. This card is one of the most neutral in the deck in terms of positive or negative associations—it's all about receiving just rewards for what you (or someone else) have been putting forth. In other words, what Justice means is all up to what you've been doing lately.

Justice is depicted as a woman on a throne—one made out of stone that doesn't look particularly comfortable, but it gets the job done, which is all Justice is after. She sits upright with both arms outstretched, wearing a flowing robe that gives her a regal bearing. Justice isn't one to be trifled with, but she isn't putting on airs, either. She has earned her place here, just as whoever stands before her throne awaiting judgement has earned theirs.

In her left hand, a sword that points towards the sky, symbolizing swift decisions and acting upon them. Once Justice determines what's fair, that's the law. In her right hand, pointed towards the ground, she holds a set of scales, symbolizing balance and an equal consequence for equal action. The positioning of her hands is a callback to our friend The Magician, in that she's connected to what's above and what's below—here, too, we have a balance.

When Justice comes up, it generally means the conditions are ripe for a situation in your life to reach a state of balance and fairness. If you've been working hard to achieve a goal, you may see a reward for that hard work. It doesn't always mean you're going to get that promotion, but you may see some recognition in equal measure to the work you've put in thus far. On the other hand, if you've been slacking off or if you've acted less than kindly lately, you can expect that you're going to reap the fruits of those actions, too. Justice is, in its essence, a card of cause and effect. It's a good reminder to stop and think about what energy and action you put out into the world, lest it return to you.

Journal Questions for Justice

• How do you feel looking at the Justice card? What sticks out about the image, and why might that be?

• What does the word "justice" mean for you? How has this idea shown up in your life in the past?

• Are you someone who believes it's your job to issue out tit-for-tat, or do you trust the Universe to balance the scales in the end? How has this impacted you?

• What seeds have you been sowing lately? When you consider your time and the energy you've been putting out into the world, what might you expect to reap from those efforts? If you don't like the answer, what needs to happen to change that?

• Can you think of a time when you experienced swift justice for something that you did? Reflect on that time and any lessons you can draw from it.

CHAPTER 14

XII: The Hanged Man

The first time I visited the Pittsburgh Renaissance Festival, I bought a one-card Tarot reading. Inside the envelope, there was no note or explanation—just a simple, Rider-Waite-Smith Tarot card—The Hanged Man. Even without a reader to interpret the card for me, I knew it was apt. That was a period of great stasis in my life, as I grappled with and tried to navigate a fresh grief. To this day, when I see The Hanged Man, I think about this version of myself.

The Hanged Man hangs from a T-shaped beam by a single foot. The other leg is crossed in a pose that seems almost relaxed. The rope that holds him there doesn't look particularly tight or secure. We get the sense that, while the figure is hanging out in stasis, it's at least partly a choice. He wouldn't have to work too hard to get free off that single rope around his ankle, yet there he hangs in a pose of near-rest, arms tucked behind his back, foot crossed.

The beam from which The Hanged Man is suspended isn't a stark, sparse bit of wood. Rather, there is some greenery growing here. We get a sense of life and motion. Even if this person is on pause right now, the world around them continues to bloom, ripe for rejoining when he's ready.

A halo of light around his head reminds one of the Sun, and it's clear that while the Hanged Man is still, his mind is active. Perhaps this flipped perspective is necessary right now in order to get a different viewpoint on a particular situation. You don't want to hang upside down like this for too long, but it may be valuable to take a look around while you're here.

When The Hanged Man shows up for you, it often indicates a period of pause or surrender. Perhaps you, too, are navigating grief like I was that day at the Renaissance Festival. Or maybe you're at the point of making a big life change, but you're not quite ready to take the leap yet. Whatever the reason may be, this period of stasis may well challenge what you thought you knew about life. It's an invitation (sometimes a forceful, sudden one) to change your perspective and see things from a different point of view. What can you learn from having your life flipped upside down before you untie that loose knot and set things right again?

Journal Questions for The Hanged Man

• When you look at the figure of The Hanged Man, what sticks out to you? How does his posture seem—relaxed, tense? How does this relate to how you feel when looking at this card?

• Think about a period of stasis or pause in your life. How did it feel to be in that moment of stillness? Did you resist it, or were you able to settle in and consider what you could learn from it?

• Are you in The Hanged Man pose in an area of your life right now? Consider where you might be in a standstill, or where you might benefit from a change of perspective.

• How do you know when it's time to get back down? Consider what information you need or perspective you need to gain while you're upside down in order to move on and improve the situation at hand.

• If you aren't in a moment of pause or stasis right now, The Hanged Man might be telling you it's time for a bit of reflection. Take a moment and consider what in your life might need a bit more consideration before you move forward.

CHAPTER 15

XIII: Death

Ah, yes, the Death card. This is undeniably pop culture's favorite card to misconstrue, as it is so often used as an ill-omen of actual, physical death. Of course, pulling a card with the title Death can be a scary experience, but this card isn't really here to tell you the grim reaper is coming for you in a literal sense. The Death card is a metaphorical death, a change or transformation that's coming in your life. This is a card I don't personally see often in the readings I do for myself—when I have encountered a change in the past, it's come by way of the Tower—a big, unexpected whammy. The Death card, on the other hand, feels a bit more like an end from natural causes, something a bit more anticipated and a bit less shocking, generally speaking (though not always).

In the archetypical illustration, the Death card features a

skeleton in armor, riding a horse and bearing a banner. He is coming to claim what has passed on, carrying that which has died away with him. Below his horse, there is indeed a deceased figure, perhaps a royal if the crown that has fallen from their head is any indication. This is a representation of that which has come to an end, and which will now be claimed by the skeleton of Death.

The figures before him are pleading, presumably begging him not to take away their beloved. But pleading with the spector of Death is useless, as is resisting change and transition when they've already come into your life. All you can do is let the past be the past and move forward, as represented by the banner that Death carries here. When a ruler like the one on the card dies, they are replaced with a new one. So, too, will whatever has fallen away from your life be replaced with someone new.

Death can be a tough card to hang with, but it's ultimately a more positive card than common misconceptions would have you believe. Change and transition, while not easy, are inevitable and important parts of life. This card lets you know that something is ending, but that also means something is beginning. Perhaps you're about to quit or lose your job, or a relationship is coming to an end. There may well be a period of mourning in store when that happens, but it means you'll be able to find a new (perhaps better) job, partner, etc. When Death comes up, let yourself mourn the endings, but know there's always an opportunity hidden within them, too.

Journal Questions for Death

• When you look at this card, what stands out to you? Which figure(s) in the card do you most relate to at this point in your life, and why?

• What is your relationship to endings? Think back on previous times when something has "died" in your life and how you handled it. What can you learn from these past experiences?

• What in your life is ready for a change or transition? Is there an area of your life that's ready for a natural ending or one that has already come to an end?

• Consider where there might be opportunity on your horizon. If something has come to an end, or if you are feeling ready to end something on your own terms, consider what space this opens up in your life. What can replace that which has died?

• If this card is hard for you, that's completely natural. If you're resistant to the idea of Death as change and transition, take a moment to consider why that is. Are you clinging to cultural representations of this card as a dangerous omen, or are you perhaps really afraid of change itself?

CHAPTER 16

Seek Balance with Temperance

XIV: Temperance

One of my favorite sayings is, "Everything in moderation… including moderation." It's tough to track down the exact origins of this phrase, which makes frequent rounds on social media these days, but it's most commonly attributed to Oscar Wilde. No matter where it comes from, it's a good saying to go along with Temperance. This card is all about balance and moderation in life, about staying steady and not over (or under) doing it.

The visual image for Temperance has a lot going on. The figure on the card appears angelic at first glance with their big, beautiful wings, but a glance down at their feet reveals hooves that remind one more of a demon. This is a good reminder that the devil started out as an angel, and there's balance in having both angels and demons in the world (think of the whole "devil on one shoulder, angel on the other" image).

One of their cloven feet is standing on water, while the other stands on a small island of earth—again, we have a sense of balance, of equilibrium between these elements.

In their hands, our Temperance angel holds two cups, which are pouring into one another apparently simultaneously. Neither cup is giving or receiving more than they can or should—the flow of water is in a steady equilibrium, and none of it spills out as a result.

In the background of the card, we see a path that leads away into the mountains, a reminder that life is a journey, and we will travel through many situations along the way, some good and some bad. A crown in the distance floats above the mountains, symbolizing keeping your goals in mind along the way in order to reach that crowning moment of celebration.

When the Temperance card shows up, it's an invitation to take stock of the balance (or lack thereof) in your life. How is that illusory work/life balance going? What about your close relationships—have you been giving or taking more than the other person lately? Temperance is a reminder to think about moderation and restoring equilibrium. Even if you can't *always* give and take in equal measure, where can you make some efforts to balance the scales? If you've been giving too much to work, can you use some of that PTO? If you're taking too much from your partner because you're exhausted, can you show them you appreciate their work by doing something small in return?

Journal Questions for Temperance

• There is so much to dig into with the imagery of this card. Take a moment to look at it and notice what sticks out to you, and why.

• Where in your life do you tend to get knocked off balance easily? Think back over past times when you've gotten out of whack and note any patterns.

• Is there an area of your life that feels out of balance right now? Perhaps there's an area that's taking up more time and energy than its fair share. Consider how things got out of equilibrium and what—if anything—you can do to balance the scales.

• What does being balanced look like for you? Consider the different plates you juggle in life and think about a time (real or imagined) when things felt relatively balanced for you. Write it down as if it's already happening, right now, at this moment.

• Remember that saying "everything in moderation, even moderation." It's not always possible to be perfectly balanced all the time. Maybe something is out of balance, and you feel it has to stay that way for a little while (for instance, you *have* to put in that overtime because you've got bills to pay). If that's the case, take some time to reflect on what you can do in other areas of your life to keep your cup filled until you're able to sort things out again.

XV: The Devil

I've always loved that The Devil comes right after Temperance in the Major Arcana, because it feels so... true. Just when you've got everything in perfect harmony, something tempting comes along to throw you off your game. That's The Devil, whispering in your ear and leading you down the path towards temptation.

In the Rider-Waite-Smith rendition, The Devil figure takes up well over two-thirds of the card, looming large the way temptation will do when we're really in its sway. Interestingly enough, The Devil's hands are in a similar pose to what we recognize from The Magician and Justice—as above, so below. His right hand reaches up in a familiar Vulcan salute, while his right hand is facing down, loosely clutching a flaming torch. The Devil, like our most magical selves, has a connection to what's above and what's below. He may not have our best interests at heart, but it doesn't mean he doesn't know what he's doing when he tempts us.

The Devil is perched on a small block, to which two naked human-like figures are tied. These figures wear thin chains around their necks and stand in a relatively easy posture. It doesn't look quite like they're being tortured or like it would be all that difficult for them to break free and run off if they wanted to. We get the sense that they're perhaps here at least partly of their own free will or that they've made a trade-off that feels worth it, and they're down to serve their sentence. Either way, they aren't *quite* human, each having small horns on their heads and tails, suggesting that they're under the sway of the underworld now that they're here, becoming increasingly enmeshed in whatever addiction or ill-begotten tendencies brought them here.

At its core, The Devil isn't about evil, per se, even if that figure is associated with it in our cultural understandings. Rather, it's a card about the dangers of temptation, addiction, and tendencies toward getting too attached to all the wrong things. When The Devil comes up, it's an invitation to consider our vices and bad habits. Have they begun to loom a bit overlarge in our lives like the devil figure on this card? Have we been giving into our most basic instincts without much consideration for the consequences? If so, this card isn't just a reminder about the dangers of lingering too long with bad habits—it's a reminder that we could slip those chains and make a break for it if we put the effort in.

A note: true addiction is a real and serious struggle, and I don't mean to suggest that it's a simple thing to leave behind. But you can reach out to get help and start the process.

Journal Questions for The Devil

• Which figure do you identify with in the image of The Devil card? Are you one of the human-ish figures, or do you feel a bit more like the Devil? Why?

• What comes to mind when you think about temptation? What are your bad habits or vices from the past (or present), and how have they impacted you?

• Have there been times in life when leaning into temptation felt like the right answer, or seemed to work out in your favor? Examine these moments. Were they truly positive? Are your vices actually holding you back, or are you being too hard on yourself?

• What would it mean to break loose from the chains? What would you need to do to get free, and what does that freedom look like? Is it moderation, or is it total cold turkey quitting your bad habit?

• Make a list of the reasons why you don't want to lean into temptation too much in the future. Consider the impact your more basic tendencies have had on you and why you want to moderate them in the future. Come back to the list the next time The Devil card comes knocking.

CHAPTER 18

XVI: The Tower

Ah, yes, The Tower. This is without a doubt the card I fear the most, even though I follow the "there are no bad cards" philosophy of Tarot. This card is all about swift, sudden change, often leaving turmoil in its wake. I pulled it the day my supervisor got fired and the department I worked in got restructured, and I pulled it countless times in the weeks leading up to the start of the COVID-19 pandemic (as did many Tarot readers, if the online chatter is to be believed). This card isn't about small or incremental change—it's a "burn it all down" kind of vibe, and often times you're not the one doing the burning. Like the lightning strike from the card's image, The Tower change tends to come from an outside force when you least expect it.

The imagery of The Tower card is clear in its meaning. A tower is lit aflame, struck by a sudden burst of lightning that's knocked its crown-shaped roof right off. An outside force of nature has come in, disrupting what once seemed like a solid structure, and all anyone inside can do is live with the consequences.

In the foreground, figures fall from the burning tower. One appears to have leapt based on the way they fall face forward, arms outstretched. The other figure, on the other hand, looks more like they've fallen out backwards. The message here seems to be that once change comes for you, you've got two choices—jump into the change and try to direct what's next, or let it throw you overboard without a life raft. Either way, you can't stay in the tower—it's on fire, and it's crashing to the ground.

When The Tower comes up, my first instinct is to tell you to brace yourself. Prepare for the unexpected as best you can, and get ready to pivot from the plan because the plan might change right under your feet. But there *is* a positive side to this card, and a lesson, as well. Sometimes we need to get shaken up in order to break free of a rut. Sometimes, The Tower comes up when we're stuck in a situation that isn't serving us, but we're not taking any action to get ourselves out. So, the Universe takes matters into its own hands and forces us out of that situation. Maybe you're stuck in a job that's left you burnt out and frustrated, coming home in tears most of the time, but you're comfortable there and can't see yourself quitting. Bam! The Tower comes in, and suddenly, you're part of company-wide layoffs. A terrible, unexpected occurrence, to be sure, but one that's forced you out of the terrible job that was crushing you. Ultimately, that's what The Tower is about—what we're able to make of the wreckage when sudden changes come down.

Journal Questions for The Tower

• What comes to mind when you look at the image of The Tower? Do you relate to the figures falling from the building, and if so, which one? Or maybe you've made a big decision, and you feel a little bit more like the lightning strike.

• Consider one or more Tower moments from your past. It may be painful to reflect on the sudden changes that have come for us, but it can be helpful to remember that we did get through them. Spend some time considering how you navigated these swift changes and what, if anything, it taught you or gave you in return.

• Take that same moment from the second question, or consider another Tower moment that comes to mind. Now that the dust has cleared, what do you have in your life that you wouldn't have if things had stayed the same? In what ways did being forced to rebuild improve or alter your life in meaningful ways?

• Where in your life are you stagnant or in need of change? Consider the places that could use some shaking up and whether you're in a position to make those changes before life makes them for you.

• If the Tower is coming up for you, sometimes you're already in the midst of upheaval. If so, take some time to reflect on what's going on and how you can respond to it. What might you be able to build in your life when the smoke clears, and how can you set that foundation now?

CHAPTER 19

XVII: The Star

The Star card is like seeing the twinkle of a single star against a night sky—it's a glimmer of hope, a promise that somewhere out there, more glittering orbs exist, even if you can't see them right this moment. It comes after The Tower for a reason, as a reminder that there is generally always hope, however fragile it may be.

The Star card overflows nourishment and restoration. It depicts a naked woman standing before a stream, two jugs of water in her hands. One jug goes into the stream, refilling it, while the other waters the ground itself. In this way, she restores both earth and water, keeping these elements in balance. Her cups quite literally runneth over, and using them to restore the world around her ensures that she will continue to receive fertile rewards from it in the future. She has one foot on land and one in the pool of water, symbolizing balance within her emotional and practical sides (water represents emotion, and earth represents the physical world, remember).

Behind her, we see lush greenery, showing how her gifts have helped support this ecosystem. A bird perches on a tree, watching her. In the sky behind her, seven small stars twinkle, with an eighth massive star in the center of the card. These stars could be read as representing the seven energy centers/chakras, which seem to be in alignment here. We could also see the central star as the sun itself, nurturing the Earth. Either way, there's a sense that all here is as it should be, at least for the moment.

When you pull The Star, it's time to look for the silver linings to your storm clouds. Things may or may not feel particularly bright and shiny right now, but this card is here to remind you that there's always something positive, some ray of hope for the future that you can grasp. Look for it and grab your metaphorical water jug to start giving it the support it needs to thrive.

Journal Questions for The Star

• Sit with the imagery of The Star for a moment. What sticks out to you about this card? Why do you think you're drawn to those symbols or images?

• What are the "stars" in your life right now? Take a moment to jot down what's going well or what you are grateful for, however small.

• If it feels difficult to find bright moments right now, be gentle with yourself. Try to reflect on bright spots from the past or what you hope to manifest in the future. As you reflect, consider whether thinking about past and future gratitude allows you to see what's good in the present moment.

• What are you watering in your life right now? Where is your energy going, and is that where you'd like to focus your efforts? If not, how might you realign so you are able to devote more energy to nourishing what you want to flourish in your life?

• What is your North Star, the guiding light you're heading towards? When you think of navigating life, what is it that shows you the way when you're feeling lost?

CHAPTER 20

XVIII: The Moon

As a kid, I loved The Moon and felt a deep connection to it without really knowing or asking myself why. When I started learning about Tarot, I'll admit I was a little bit offended to realize The Moon isn't one of the cheeriest cards in the deck.

We're going to talk a little bit about what The Moon card typically means, at least as I interpret it. But before we do, I'd encourage you to look at the imagery on whichever version of The Moon card you've got in front of you. What do you see in the image, and how does it make you feel? Do particular symbols stick out to you? Jot this down now and return to it as you reflect on the card using the journal questions below.

In the Rider-Waite-Smith depiction, the moon looks down over tumultuous waters. It's got a bit of a stern look on its face, as though frustrated by what it's seeing. There's a sense of duality in the surrounding images–two towers in the distance on either side, a dog and a wolf howling at the moon, and depictions of land and sea. In the forefront, a lobster crawls from the water onto the land, bridging the distance between two worlds. As I see it, this card is inviting us to consider that there are two sides to every coin, that we all contain the domesticated dog and the wild wolf.

At its core, The Moon is about what we reflect to ourselves and the outside world, and whether we're being honest about who we say we are. It's a card of deception, of the hidden and lurking meanings that hide within all of us. Whether you're concealing things from yourself or from others, this card is a reminder that nothing remains hidden for long. It's an invitation to get honest with ourselves so we can step into our truth. In other words, she's got some hard lessons for us, but they're worth learning.

When working with the energy of the Moon card, we've got to get comfortable with knowing that no one is 100% honest all the time. We're all trying to put our best foot forward, and sometimes that means using a filter on social media or embellishing our resume to get the dream job. But, dishonesty never serves us in the long run, and The Moon wants to invite us to live a more authentic version of our lives.

Journaling with this card means digging deep into the stories we tell ourselves and one another, then asking, "Is it true?" These questions are an invitation to reflect on the energies of the Moon card. Use them when you pull The Moon in a one-card reading, or any time reflecting on the notion of illusion and hidden things may call to you. The Moon is a great card to reflect on when engaging in shadow work and trying to understand what you might be hiding from, even within yourself.

Journal Questions for The Moon

• Return to the imagery of this card (or reflect on it for the first time). What sticks out to you about this card? How do the images make you feel? Do they remind you of anything?

• What are you keeping hidden from others? From yourself?

• What is your relationship to truth and honesty? Do you find yourself concealing too much? Revealing too much?

• Reflect on your relationship to dreams. Do you remember your dreams? If so, what might they be telling you?

• Consider your relationship to the moon in general, the ebbing and flowing energies of that mysterious orb in the sky. Do you pay attention to its cycles and work with them? If so, take a moment to reflect on how that's been serving you. Perhaps The Moon is coming forth to invite you to work with its energies.

XIX: The Sun

When I see The Sun card, it feels a bit like a promise that I'm about to have a great day. Of course, nothing is promised, so it doesn't *always* mean this. Still, it's one of the most cheerful and bright cards in the Tarot, which isn't surprising considering its name.

The image on the Rider-Waite-Smith version of the card brings these sunshine vibes to the forefront. In the top half of the image, we have The Sun, with a passive, calm expression on its face and rays that extend beyond what we can see. The sunshine and its rays are abundant and radiate outward, which explains why the field of sunflowers below is in such effusive bloom. They have been showered with the life-giving rays of The Sun, and they're showing it.

In the foreground of the image, we have a naked baby riding a horse. The infant's arms are spread wide in open, earnest joy. The horse also appears to be smiling, as if it enjoys the child's presence. This shows the bright, clear willingness to accept life's gifts that we often have before we're old enough to learn distrust or scarcity. There's a nice feather in this kid's cap, as well, so we get the sense they have everything they need and more.

When The Sun shows up, it's an invitation to welcome fun into your life and embrace the joy that comes your way. No, it doesn't always mean that everything in life is rose-tinted and harmonious, but it's a good reminder that we enjoy life more when we take a break from taking it so darn seriously. When you pull The Sun, try connecting to your inner child a bit. Stop to smell the flowers or feel the sun on your skin. Let those positive vibes sink in wherever they can. Things are good, or at least *some* of them are.

Journal Questions for The Sun

• Look at your version of The Sun card. What images or items are you drawn to, and what do they mean to you?

• Think back on your child self. Who were you before you grew into society's expectations of you? What did you like to do? What made you laugh and smile? Can you bring any of these things back into your life?

• Maybe things don't feel so sunny and bright right now, and you're feeling frustrated at seeing this card when you're more The Cloud than The Sun. First, that's okay! Take a moment to journal on why you feel this way. Let yourself feel your feelings.

• Now, reflect on where you can see a little bit of light in life. Take some time to sit with that, too.

• What areas of your life could use a little more sunshine (aka nurturing, life-giving energy)? Where can you send more light to help grow an aspect of your life or yourself that has been left a little untended lately?

CHAPTER 22

Uncover Your Assumptions with Judgement

XX: Judgement

No one likes to be judged, which can make Judgement a bit of a scary card to pull. I'll confess that with its heavy Christian-inspired "Judgement Day" imagery, the traditional depiction of this card isn't my favorite. But, the image is apt since Judgement is a card about reflecting on whether you're living life in alignment with your higher purpose. Like the dead rising from their graves to be judged for entry to heaven, you're asked to consider whether you are living in your Truth and according to your values.

Judgement features an angel in the top half of the card, blowing a trumpet to awaken the dead below. The angel is larger than life, taking up far more space than the small humans below, showing that the spiritual life here outweighs the physical one.

The people below are all naked, having freshly risen from their coffins with arms outstretched. They appear eager and joyous, ready to welcome the Judgement from on high. We can't say for sure, but it doesn't look like there's much fear here, as if each person is confident they'll be found worthy.

When you pull Judgement, it can mean that you're in a space for inner growth. Now is a good time to reflect on your spiritual life and your values to ensure you're living in alignment with them. It may be that you haven't had much of a spiritual life to speak of but are feeling drawn to figuring out what connects you to a sense of higher power and/or bigger meaning in your life.

This may mean you're being pulled towards a big change in your life in order to shift to this new way of thinking or into better alignment with what you've really always believed. Given that the people on the card are not alone, this may include joining or deepening connections with a community that shares your beliefs or goals.

Journal Questions for Judgement

• How does the imagery of this card strike you? Where—if at all—do you see yourself in this card?

• What brings meaning to your life right now? Are there particular goals, actions, or ways of being that light you up with a sense of rightness? How can you dig deeper into these aspects of your life?

• What is your relationship to the notion of meaning or higher power in life? It's a big, kind of scary question, but this card invites you to ask it.

• What do you hope to achieve in this life so that you can greet the horn of Judgement with open arms?

• Is there a big change you've felt drawn to make in your life recently? Or perhaps you've already made that change. Take some time to reflect on what it means to shift in this way, and how it has impacted you thus far or will impact you in the future.

XXI: The World

The World is the final card in The Fool's Journey laid out in the Major Arcana, which means it's all about celebrating how far you've come and what you've achieved. This card is the pause at a high point or natural conclusion to one part of your life, before you inevitably begin again as The Fool.

The World is a satisfyingly balanced card in the Rider-Waite-Smith tradition. We have a figure floating gracefully in the center of the card, holding one wand in each hand. These bring to mind the Magician, suggesting that what was started all the way back at the beginning has now come to completion. All is in alignment and as it should be—for the moment. The figure is draped loosely in a flowing sash, another image that brings celebrations and victory to mind.

Around them is a wreath tied at top and bottom with the infinity symbol. A sense of completion but also a reminder that the circle has no end and no beginning—it will continue on and on.

In each corner of the card, a different figure is depicted as an image in the clouds, similar to those we see on the Wheel of Fortune. They represent the four elements, here in balance for the moment.

The World is a wonderful card to pull, an invitation to take a moment to pat yourself on the back. When this card appears, it reminds you to pause and take stock of how far you've come. Maybe you don't *feel* like you're in a big moment of harmonious accomplishment right now, and yet, undoubtedly, you've come pretty far from where you began in life or on this particular leg of your journey. When you see this card, take a moment to look back and find the things worth celebrating. Give yourself a moment to just rest on your laurels for once before you get back to the grind—most of us don't do this enough.

Journal Questions for Judgement

• Spend a moment with the image of The World. How does it strike you? What aspects of the imagery stick out to you, and why might that be?

• Make a list of what you've accomplished recently and take a moment to just celebrate and congratulate yourself. This can feel awkward if you're not used to patting yourself on the back, but do it anyway. It's good to celebrate yourself sometimes.

• What does it mean to feel in balance and content for you? When you consider The World's meaning as a moment of completion and celebration, what comes to mind?

• Thinking back on your answer to the previous question, do you feel like you're there now, or is that sense of accomplishment always just out of reach? If so, why might that be?

• If you do feel like you've hit a high point or the end of one chapter, The World can also be a great time to reflect on what comes next. Where might you focus your energies now that you've achieved what you wanted from this leg of your journey? When next you embody The Fool, what might that look like?

Section Two: The Minor Arcana

The Minor Arcana are generally considered the more "everyday" cards, in that they depict smaller moments compared to the major life events often represented in the Major Arcana. As we covered in the first chapter, the Minor Arcana cards are divided into four suits, much like a traditional deck of playing cards.

In a traditional Rider-Waite-Smith style deck, The Minor Arcana Suits are wands, swords, cups, and pentacles (sometimes called coins). Many decks re-interpret these suits to fit the theme (I have one that uses Dungeons & Dragons skills like strength and charisma, for instance). Even so, most decks generally still share similar enough correlations that you can use this book with any deck—just use your judgement and your guidebook to determine which suits line up with the ones in your deck.

Within each suit, there are numbered cards ranging from 1-10. Then, you have four court cards, typically a Page, Knight, Queen, and King (again, some decks get creative with these names, but the associations tend to be similar).

Like The Fool's Journey, you can trace a narrative from the one card to the 10 card in each suit, where a one tends to represent a fresh start or new beginning and a 10 tends to represent completion or the end of a given cycle. As you'll see, there are a lot of ups and downs in between, but they're generally more minor day-to-day changes rather than big ones.

Court Cards, on the other hand, are often considered to represent people related to the situation, whether it be a colleague, friend, parent, or even yourself. This isn't always the case, but it is worth noting when you pull a court card to see whether it might be trying to call your attention to a particular person in your life.

We'll journey through each of the cards in the Minor Arcana just as we did the Major Arcana, because these cards are just as important and useful for readings and self-reflection.

CHAPTER 24

Wade Into Your Feelings with The Cups

As a suit, the Cups are associated with the element of water. This makes sense when you consider the purpose of a cup or chalice—holding liquid. Because water is associated with emotions, this suit generally traces your inner emotional life and invites you to reflect on your feelings. They are also considered to be related with your subconscious and dreams.

As a Pisces who nearly always have Big Feelings about even the smallest of things, the Cups come up for me quite a lot in my personal readings. I'm partial to them as a result because they feel comfortable and familiar. In this section, we'll take a look at each of the numbered cards in the Suit of Cups. We'll get to the Court Cards in the next section because they're a bit different.

Ace of Cups

The Ace of Cups, like any Ace, marks a fresh start. When you're looking at the Ace of Cups, there's generally something new going on in your emotional depths. I often think about new relationships (romantic or otherwise) when I see this card, or a new passion project.

This card depicts a hand holding an overflowing cup with streams of water flowing from within that can't be contained. It's that exciting, almost overwhelming rush of emotion you get at the start of a new relationship or venture. Beneath the cup, the water pools into a pond dotted with lotus leaves. This shows the depth of feeling available to us as human beings, and can also represent the subconscious, particularly if you've been working with dreams or doing Shadow Work lately.

There's a dreamlike quality to this card in that the hand holding the cup is shrouded in clouds, giving it a mystical vibe. This implies that there could be a spiritual element to what's going on right now, and the new thing you've fallen in love with may be a spiritual path or practice.

A bird, most often depicted as a dove, dives towards the cup. If we think about the symbol of the dove in the Christian story of Noah and the Ark, it can be seen as representing a positive sign or blessing from the heavens. Doves are also associated with peace, so in general the dove's presence here means that this card is generally perceived as a positive one. That doesn't mean whatever's just beginning will stay that way, but right now you're in that fresh, rose-tinted beginning phase.

When I pull the Ace of Cups, I generally check in to see what I'm excited about, what energizes me, and gives me the "first-date" butterfly feeling.

Journal Questions for the Ace of Cups

• What comes to mind when you see that cup overflowing? What feels abundant in bringing you joy at this point in your life?

• What is beginning or feeling fresh in your emotional life at this moment? Is there a new relationship, project, or hobby that is sparking positive feelings for you right now?

• If something new has come into your life, take a moment to reflect on how that makes you feel. Is it full of excitement and joy, or do you also tend to be a bit anxious or afraid of change even when that change is positive?

• If you're not feeling a sense of newness or excitement, this card might be a reminder to change your perspective. If things are feeling stale, what can you do to re-invigorate your excitement and energy for the things you value?

• Let's say you resonate more with the cup overflowing as an emotional overload than an overflow of positive feelings. What can you do to get things back under control so that your emotions feel manageable? What helps when you're feeling too many feelings?

CHAPTER 26

Embrace Companionship with the
Two of Cups

Two of Cups

Twos in Tarot often represent duality, choosing between or balancing two things. With the Two of Cups, though, we are most often looking at the emotional balance of two human beings in their relationship with one another. Often, this card signifies romantic relationships, but it could also align with a friendship, business partnership, or other situation that involves working closely with another person.

In the classic image for the Two of Cups, two individuals stand facing one another with their hands clasped. It's something of a marriage/union vibe, as they seem prepared to drink from their cups. Both partners take up an equal amount of space on the card, and their cups are of equal size, symbolizing that this is a balanced partnership. In the Two of Cups, both parties are getting something out of this union, and they're glad to be in partnership.

Above our couple, a symbol hangs in the sky, depicting a staff with two snakes wrapped around it. This is a symbol of trade and partnerships, again reinforcing that the union depicted here may not always be a romantic one, but could well symbolize a business deal or work relationship. The Lion's head atop is a symbol of fiery Leo, which indicates passion—whether that passion is of the sensual variety in a love match or that of shared enthusiasm for a project or idea.

Behind the couple are gently rolling green hills, the universal symbol of fertility and prosperity. Good things will come from this union.

When you pull the Two of Cups, it's a good time to reflect on the partnerships in your life. Who is helping you achieve your goals, or who might you align yourself with? If you've been thinking about a new business partner or saying yes to a date with that person you're curious about, this card might indicate that your instincts are correct on this one—go for it! On the other hand, this card might be a reminder to examine existing relationships and see how you can bring them back into this aligned state if they've left it behind.

Journal Questions for the Two of Cups

• What does the imagery on your version of the Two of Cups card evoke for you? What stands out, and why do you think you are drawn to those images?

• Take a moment to reflect on the partnerships in your life at this moment. Where are they in balance? Where might they be off kilter? What actions, if any, can you take to bring things back into harmony?

• If one of your relationships is terribly off balance and you're struggling to see how to bring it into harmony, you may want to examine why this relationship still exists in your life. Is this a person you want to remain in partnership with, or is it time to cut ties?

• What is your relationship to the idea of partnership in general? Do you feel comfortable sharing your life with someone, or do you prefer to go solo? Why might that be?

• If there is a new partnership or relationship you're considering entering into, take a moment to consider what you want to get out of that relationship. Will this person be able to serve those needs for you at this time to the best of your knowledge? Will you?

Three of Cups

The Three of Cups is a beautiful card to pull, because it is all about gathering with and celebrating your community. I always smile when I see this one, as it's an invitation to remember the people who add meaning and joy to our lives.

In the image for the classic rendition of the Three of Cups, three women dance together in a circle, their cups raised high in a toast to joy and friendship. The women wear long flowing robes, adding to the air of comfort and celebration. The field in which they dance is ripe with grapes, flowers, and a pumpkin, showing that there is indeed much to celebrate right now for these women.

This card, more than anything, is one for celebration and gratitude. It is a call to join with your community and make some time for joy. It might even be a good idea to gather together to create something artistic, as the Three of Cups can also symbolize creativity with the fertile fields bursting forth with the fruit of ideas.

Journal Questions for the Three of Cups

• What comes to mind for you when you see the image of the Three of Cups? Jot down any particular images that you feel drawn to or which provoke a strong reaction.

• When was the last time you gathered to celebrate and experience community? If it's been a while, are you in a position to plan something and create a space for gathering?

• Sometimes, this card can be a tough one, if we are far away from our community or separated from them in other ways. If you have a person or people you can't access in person, what are some other ways you might celebrate and create a virtual or long-distance community? Or, how might you find and call in a new community where you are right now?

• If being around other people doesn't feel great right now, or if you're unable to access a community, how might you bring some solo celebration into your life? What can you do to make the day feel special, even if it's shared just with yourself?

• Maybe this card is coming up because you're just so full of ideas you can barely contain your excitement. If so, take some time to just free-write those ideas. Let them come to life on paper, with no judgement, no consideration of how realistic they are. Just be with that enthusiasm and creativity for a little while.

CHAPTER 28

Four of Cups

The Four of Cups, in essence, tells us that now is the time to sit down and think. It's a card of contemplation and reflection, telling us that now might not be the time to take on a slew of new opportunities and charge ahead. Rather, we need to take stock of what *is* before we keep working towards what's *next*.

The Four of Cups shows a figure sitting under a tree with their arms and legs crossed. It is a very "no, thank you" kind of vibe they're giving off even as a hand emerges from a cloud to offer up an enticing new cup full of opportunities. The figure in the card, though, would rather stare at and reflect on the three cups already before them before saying *yes* to taking on anything else. It could well be that what they've got in their three cups is more than enough for the time being.

When this card comes up, I see it as a reminder to revisit your boundaries and priorities. Where is your time and energy going, and is there enough to go around? Before you say *yes* to being helpful or because it seems like a good opportunity, take stock of whether you have the space to invite something new in right now. It could be that you need to realign with your priorities and trim something else away before you're in a space to invite new things into your life.

Journal Questions for the Four of Cups

• Take a look at this card's image. What about it sticks out or resonates with you? Why might that be?

• What is your relationship to saying "no"? Do you tend to overcommit even when you're too busy? If so, why might that be, and how has it served you in the past?

• Maybe saying "no" is easy for you... perhaps even too easy? If you're in a space where "no" is your default, try to slow down a little bit and consider what opportunities you might be missing.

• What are your priorities in life? Take a moment to consider what is important to you, and what you value. It's important to check in on these priorities from time to time before we can even really consider whether we're living in alignment with them.

• What's on your plate (or in your cups) right now? Take a moment to consider your responsibilities and to-do lists. Now ask yourself how this aligns with your priorities. If there's a gap here, take some time to consider if you can bring things into better alignment.

CHAPTER 29

Five of Cups

Ah, yes, the Five of Cups. Not the happiest of cards upon first glance, with all the spilled cups, but I think this card actually brings a positive message. Things are not as bad as you think, and while there may be something to mourn in your life right now, that doesn't mean there isn't anything to be grateful for, too.

In the Five of Cups, a figure stands with their shoulders hunched, a thick cloak draped over them. They stand on the side of the road, off their path, and look down in apparent despair at the three spilled cups that lay before them. What a tragedy, to lose all the liquid in those cups... and yet, if the figure would just turn around, they'd see that they still have two upright cups that are still very much full.

In other words, this card wants you to stop moping about what you've lost and turn your attention back to what's going *right*. The Five of Cups does often reflect a time of loss or grief, and it's perfectly reasonable and valid to take a moment to sit with and let yourself feel that grief. Just know there's still good to be seen, if only you turn around and look. So, feel your sadness and mourn that which you've lost... just don't do it at the expense of the good things that are still present in your life.

Journal Questions for the Five of Cups

• When you see the image on your version of this card, what draws your attention, and why?

• Do you have some spilled cups you've been crying over? Take a few moments to honor that grief. Write down what you've lost and why it was important to you.

• Now, let's look at those cups on the other side. What is still going well? What can you be grateful for and continue to nurture in this difficult moment?

• If you still need some help looking on the upside, try reflecting back on previous times when you found yourself focused on what you'd lost. Were things really as bad as they seemed, now that you are looking back on it from the future?

• Continuing to reflect on a past Five of Cups moment from your life, take some time to think about what helped you get through the difficult moments. Can you apply anything from these past lessons to your current situation?

CHAPTER 30

Embrace Your Innocence with the Six of Cups

Six of Cups

The Six of Cups is all about nostalgia and looking back on childhood innocence. For some, this may not bring quite the same flowers and roses as depicted on the card, but even so, there's something special about the innocence of childhood. This card invites us to tap into our child-mind and see the world as full of fresh and vibrant opportunities.

The Six of Cups depicts a child bundled up in a thick cloak and gloves. They are padded and well-protected from the harsh realities of the world as a figure leans over to offer them a cup filled with blooming flowers. All around them, more cups with more flowers are in plain view (six in total, of course). This card evokes a sense of safety and abundance associated with the innocence of childhood.

When this card pops up, it's an invitation to see the world with a bit more of a rosy tint, embracing nostalgia or innocence. If you've been feeling stagnant or stuck, particularly in relationships with others, this is a great time to wipe the slate clean and try to start over as best you can. Just as the child in the image will accept the gift being offered, try to accept that the people in your life are offering the best they can and take it at face value.

Journal Questions for the Six of Cups

• What does the imagery on your version of this card evoke for you? What images or aspects of the card are you drawn to, and what might they represent for you?

• What might life be offering you right now if you were open enough to accept it? Take a moment to consider the people and opportunities in your life, particularly anything that could use a refresh or a fresh start.

• Take a moment to remember who you were as a child. What did you enjoy? What were your hopes and dreams? If you can, try to honor your child self in the coming days by doing an activity you used to love or working towards a childhood dream.

• What gives you a sense of safety and security in your life? If these feelings are absent, can you think of a time when you did feel safe? How might you channel some of that energy into your here and now?

• Consider your role as a caregiver. Did you feel cared for when you were small, or did you do the caring from an early age? How might that impact how you see the world today?

CHAPTER 31

Explore your Options with the Seven of Cups

Seven of Cups

Maybe it's the former literature major in me, but I can't help but think of that famous moment from Sylvia Plath's *The Bell Jar* when I see the Seven of Cups. In it, she describes feeling like she's sitting under a fig tree, paralyzed with indecision because she can't decide which fig to pick. By picking none, they all overripen and fall away, leaving her with zero figs. It's a metaphor for choosing possible futures, and it also happens to be pretty much the same message the Seven of Cups is serving. Having a lot of options can be overwhelming and lead to decision paralysis, but sometimes you *have* to choose or risk losing all those options altogether.

In the image for the Seven of Cups a silhouetted figure looks out at a cloud, where seven cups are lined up before them. Each cup contains a different, enticing treasure—a castle, a laurel wreath, a dragon, a lover, and so on. The figure leans back as though overwhelmed by their options, by the decision before them. They can't drink from every cup, but how to choose the right one?

The Seven of Cups is about overburden, about feeling pulled in so many directions you don't know where to turn. It's a reminder that we can't do or have everything all the time. You don't want to sit under that fig tree forever—you need to choose something and get moving, even if that may mean losing out on some of the other possibilities before you.

Journal Questions for the Seven of Cups

• When you see these cups full of possibilities, what do the images represent to you? Which cups are most enticing, and why do you think that is?

• Take a moment to write down the choices or decisions that lie before you right now. What is making it difficult to move forward? It may be helpful to spend some time writing out the pros and cons of different choices or even just journaling your way through the different considerations around them. The goal here isn't necessarily to make your decision right this instant, but to spend some time getting to the bottom of why you might be feeling this sense of overwhelm.

• Sometimes, the Seven of Cups can represent illusions or wishful thinking. Perhaps you don't have that many options in front of you right now, and you're counting your chickens before they hatch. Take some time to be realistic about your situation if you feel this might be you. What options are *actually* on the table right now?

• Maybe you're having the opposite of the *Bell Jar* problem, and this card is here to remind you that there's more choice available than you think. If you're feeling stuck or unsure of the way forward, take some time to jot down what possibilities you'd like to see open up for you.

• Now look at your list from question four and consider whether any of those possibilities already exist in your life. If not, is there anything you can do to invite them in?

Eight of Cups

If the Seven of Cups is about choosing something, the Eight of Cups represents walking away from that which you didn't choose. It's a card about disappointment, but specifically about moving on from and leaving behind that disappointing situation.

The Eight of Cups features eight neatly stacked cups in the foreground, taking up the bottom half of the card. I can't say for sure, but these cups always strike me as empty or lacking in some way. Would you really stack them on top of each other if they weren't? In the background, a figure with a walking stick and a cloak pulled around them walks away, their back turned to the cups. These cups represent a situation or opportunity that had to be left behind in order to move forward. The person who's walking away seems to have crossed a chasm to get where they are now, giving a sense of no return. In the sky, even the moon looks sad to see what's going on here.

When the Eight of Cups comes up for you, it often means it's time to move on. There may be a present disappointment that you've been wallowing in, or perhaps you're stuck in a situation that isn't serving you. Whatever it is, it's time to try and move on. Whether what you're mourning is something good you can't hold on to or a bad situation you need to remove yourself from, this card is your signal to grab that walking stick and get going. Wallowing or clinging to something when it's already over won't get you anywhere.

Journal Questions for the Eight of Cups

• Look at those cups in the foreground. What do they represent for you right now? What situation is taking up a lot of mental space, even if you've already left it behind?

• Now, put yourself in the shoes of the figure walking away. What are they walking towards? By leaving your past in the past, what new opportunities or possibilities are you making space to welcome into your life?

• Whatever it is you need to walk away from, perhaps you're struggling to do so from a lack of closure. We can't always get closure in life, but you can take some time to reflect on the situation, person, etc., that you need to let go of. Say your goodbyes on paper and use that time to let go. You could even burn the journal entry when you're done if you need a little extra farewell symbolism.

• If you can't think of a current situation that you need to walk away from, perhaps this card is an invitation to reflect on something from the past that's still impacting you. Have you had to leave something behind before? How did it go?

• In general, is it easy for you to tell when it's time to walk away or move on from something? Or do you struggle with staying or holding on even when a relationship or situation is well past serving you? Take some time to reflect on your patterns here and how they have served you.

to see open up for you.

• Now look at your list from question four and consider whether any of those possibilities already exist in your life. If not, is there anything you can do to invite them in?

CHAPTER 33

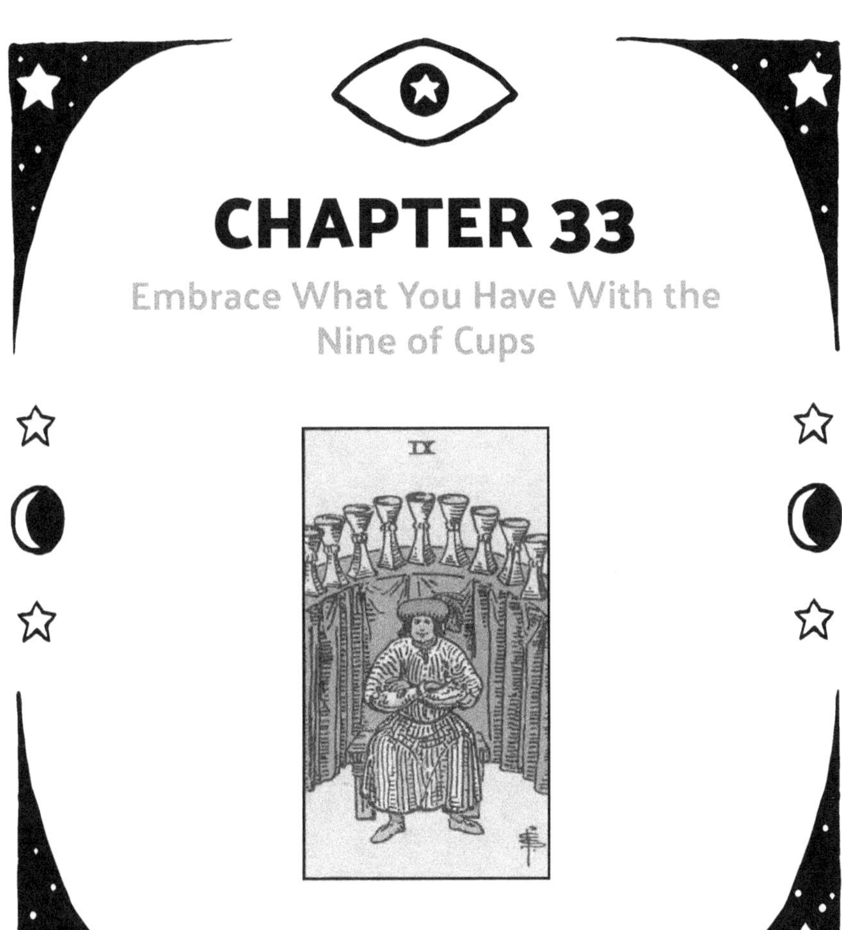

Nine of Cups

The Nine of Cups is all about taking a moment to pause and appreciate what you have. This card reflects contentment and a sense of gratitude for the abundance in your life. While we haven't fully completed our journey through the suit of cups, we've come a long way, and it's time to look back and appreciate how far we've come.

The Nine of Cups is a relatively simple image. A figure sits on a bend with their arms crossed in a pose of contentment. They wear a nice hat with a few feathers tucked into it, and a relatively simple gown or robe. Behind them is a table lined with a tablecloth, atop which sit nine neatly perched cups. This is someone who is resting, content with what they have and not actively seeking more. The cups and the relatively simple clothes are enough, at least in this moment.

When I see the Nine of Cups, it's an invitation to rest, and to pull out that gratitude journal. It's a signal that we can't *always* be striving, moving, pushing for the next big thing. Sometimes, what we need to do is sit still for a moment and appreciate what we already have.

Journal Questions for the Nine of Cups

• Can you think of a time when you felt like the figure on the Nine of Cups card? Resting easy, or, at least, taking a pause?

• Is it easy for you to rest when you need to, or do you feel the need to always be productive? If you are the type of person who wears your busy nature like a badge of honor, consider how that's been serving you.

• Let's look at those cups on the table for a moment. These represent the good things, the abundant things, in our lives. What's in your cups at the moment that makes them "half full," as the saying goes? In other words, make a gratitude list and acknowledge the things that fill your life in a positive way right now.

• Maybe you're not feeling so restful and abundant now. Take a moment to write down what rest means to you and remind yourself of why you deserve it even if you don't feel like you've achieved your Nine of Cups moment. Come back to this list whenever you're struggling to feel like you've earned or deserve moments of rest.

• There's a difference between downtime and rest. What, for you, does truly nourishing rest look like? In other words, what fills your cup?

Ten of Cups

In the Tarot suits, 10 is the number of completion. It's the last card in the Cups cycle before we get into the Court Cards (much like a standard playing card deck). Therefore, the 10s tend to represent a sense of completion or ending before the next leg of your journey begins. With the cups, this indicates a sense of emotional fulfillment or satisfaction. This card is an invitation to reflect upon and celebrate the loving relationships in your life—romantic, friendships, family, etc.

The artwork on the Ten of Cups shows a couple looking up at a shining arc created by ten cups floating in the sky. They're embracing one another, with their arms thrown out wide as if to embrace the fullness of their gratitude and emotional satisfaction in this moment. Beside them, two children (presumably the couple's offspring) dance with joy. Ahead of them are rolling fields with greenery and a nice home tucked away in the hillside. The whole image screams familial bliss and security, fitting for the message of the Ten of Cups.

When this card comes up, I always look to what's going well in my relationships. Maybe I made a new friend or had the chance to connect over video chat with an older acquaintance. Perhaps I'm feeling particularly grateful for my marriage or my family. Sometimes, this card comes up when we're not feeling particularly well-connected or satisfied with our social lives, and I think its purpose then is to remind us that things aren't as bad as we might think. Just because we may not have a romantic partner, it doesn't mean there aren't other joyful and nourishing relationships in our lives. See this card as an invitation to celebrate the love you have in your life, in whatever form it may take.

Journal Questions for the Ten of Cups

• When you look at the illustration on your version of the Ten of Cups, what images stick out? Do you see yourself in one of the figures on the card? Or perhaps you're drawn to something in the background. Take a moment to journal why you think you're drawn to that part of the card today.

• Which relationships can you express gratitude for at this moment? Who is important in your life, and how might you take a moment to acknowledge the importance of this emotional bond?

• Maybe you're not feeling it and want to bring more of that Ten of Cups energy into your life. Take a moment to jot down the types of relationships you want to foster in your life. If you're looking for a romantic partner, what do you value in that kind of relationship?

• Maybe you're not seeking a romantic relationship but, rather, seeking friends. What do you hope to gain from more friendships in your life? Write about these relationships as if they're already present in your life if you want to throw in a little extra manifestation magic.

• How do *you* like to be appreciated by the people in your life? Do you communicate to the people in your life when you need something or when they express a desire to do something nice for you?

Court Cards and the Cups

Each Tarot suit has court cards in addition to the numbered cards. These cards are the Page, Knight, Queen, and King in each suit. Many readers see the court cards as representing people in our lives—sometimes us, sometimes another individual who is influencing us at the moment. Pages often represent a beginner's mind or being a novice at something—think fresh or start-of-the-journey energy. Knights are go-getters, always going out there getting things done. Queens tend to be the feminine energy of the court cards, whereas the King is your authoritative masculine.

In the cups, these cards fit into the overall story of feelings and intuition that the cups suit is telling. Let's dig into what each of the four court cards means when it comes to the suit of Cups.

CHAPTER 35

Page of Cups

The Pages in Tarot have an echo of The Fool energy to them—they're characterized as young and often just starting out with something new. With the cups, we're looking at creative ventures and passion projects. The Page of Cups, then, represents the potential for a new creative project or idea, an opportunity. As a Pisces girl, I love this card—it reminds me to approach my creative side with a beginner's mind and step back into the wonder of childhood for a moment.

The card shows a young figure dressed in a courtly manner with a big fancy hat on their head. In one hand, they grasp a cup, and they seem to be leaning toward it. Inside the cup, a fish is sticking its head out as if it's talking to our Page. And they are leaning in to listen to whatever exciting new ideas the fish has to offer. This card, then, has magic to it, a note of inspiration from both the natural and supernatural (after all, your average fish can't talk!)

When the Page of Cups shows up, it's a good time to be on the lookout for new ideas and opportunities. Some readers see the court cards as representing people, and, in which case, this card may indicate someone with a young and creative energy in your life—it may even be you!

Journal Questions for the Page of Cups

• What stands out to you in your deck's version of the Page of Cups? Are you drawn to a particular figure or aspect of the card? What might that represent for you?

• Take a moment to consider any new ideas or opportunities that have presented themselves to you recently. What would it look like to take action on them?

• Or, if you don't think there are any new ideas or projects available to you right now, spend a moment brainstorming and see what comes to mind. Set a timer and just flow with your ideas—you never know what might come up!

• Maybe you're feeling stagnant, and this card feels like a cruel reminder of that freshness and vibrancy you aren't feeling in your life right now. What opportunities do you want to see come knocking? Jot down the types of creative projects, goals, or opportunities you want to manifest.

• When was the last time that you were truly a beginner in life? What did it feel like to start a new hobby, job, or move someplace new?

Knight of Cups

If Pages are the young, eager members of the court cards, the Knight of Cups is your twenty-something in the midst of early adulthood, full of eagerness and ambition. They're the ones going out and getting things done. If the Page is getting a new idea, the Knight is following through on it. It's the "butt in chair" aspect of creative work, the part where you do actually have to sit down to write, draw, or do whatever it is that you must to make those big creative ideas and projects actually come to fruition.

The Knight of Cups features a Knight on horseback, holding a single cup aloft. They have a sure, upright posture as they ride forth to accomplish their goals. The horse has its head bowed and its leg up, mid-stride, another sign that this court card is all about forward momentum. They are about to cross a stream, giving us a reminder that this Knight is all about intuition and creativity.

If the Knight does symbolize a person in your reading, they're quite the romantic. It may mean a new potential lover with a penchant for romance is entering the scene, or it may reflect your own tendencies to romanticize things. Either way, when you see the Knight of Cups, it's likely that big emotions and projects are afoot.

Journal Questions for the Knight of Cups

• Take a moment to reflect on your version of the Knight of Cups card. What about the image draws your attention at this moment, and why might that be?

• What's in that cup being clasped so tightly by the knight? What is the major focus or project in your life at this moment, and are you really dedicating the time and energy that you need in order to make it happen?

• If you're not dedicating the time and energy to the things that matter, why is that? Are you holding yourself back, or are other elements of life taking up your time and energy?

• What's the stream? What crossroads may you be approaching at this moment that will require careful, sure steps to cross?

• Are you a romantic, or do you tend to be more practical? Take a good look at your situation and make sure you're really seeing it clearly.

CHAPTER 37

Queen of Cups

Queens in the Tarot represent feminine, nurturing energy. In the case of the Queen of Cups, we're looking at someone who works to keep emotional needs fulfilled and balanced. This card has a very caring, maternal energy to it and could symbolize a mother figure or the need to mother yourself at this time of your life.

The Queen of Cups card traditionally depicts a woman seated on a rather elaborate throne. In her hands, she holds a large, covered cup—the only chalice in the suit that comes with a lid, for good reason. The covered cup reminds us that this is a woman who has her emotions and her intuition under control so that they serve her. Her throne sits in a lush field, facing a body of water, showing the Queen of Cups' easy connection with nature and fertility.

When the Queen of Cups come up, one of two things is likely to happen. Either you're already in a balanced emotional and intuitive state and the Tarot is giving you a pat on the back to keep it up, or you're a total emotional wreck who needs to tend to yourself before things get worse. Either way, I see this as a comforting card. It can be hard to think of nurturing maternal energy if you have an absent or unstable mother figure in your own life, but remember that *you* can meet your emotional needs and provide that nurturing energy to yourself. Now is a time to tend to your inner life and make sure you're doing what you need to stay in a solid, steady state.

Journal Questions for the Queen of Cups

• What stands out to you about your version of the Queen of Cups? What images are you drawn to or resistant to, and why do you think this is?

• How *are* you right now? Spend some time to really answer this question and connect with your emotional state.

• In general, how easy is it for you to connect to your emotions? Do you often know what you're feeling, or are you someone who has to really pause to tap into your emotional state?

• What is your relationship to big feelings? Do you get easily overwhelmed by your emotions, or do you keep a tight lid on them?

• If you pulled out the Queen of Cups to ask a complicated question that's been on your mind, there's a solid chance this card is letting you know that you've already got the answer. Take a moment to tap into what your gut is saying about this situation and write it out.

CHAPTER 38

King of Cups

The King is *in charge* when it comes to the Tarot suits. Where the Queen is a nurturing balanced state, the King is about control and mastery. When we think about the masculine approach to emotions in our culture, this makes some sense—it's about keeping things under control and not letting your emotions get the better of you. While too much of this energy isn't wise, the King comes up when you may need to exercise a bit more logic to bring yourself back into balance between your emotional heart and your logical brain.

The King of Cups, like the Queen, sits on a throne. His is less ornate, and also happens to be floating in the middle of the ocean. He holds a cup firmly in one hand and an unlit torch firmly in the other. The waves behind him look a bit chaotic, but he stands firm on his throne/ship, unconcerned because he knows that he's in control here. A ship and a fish in the background are a reminder of all that activity going on in the waters behind him, further illustrating that the King has found a way to master the chaos of emotions and intuition to serve him.

When the King comes up, it may be a sign that you've lost control of your emotional state. Perhaps you've been through it and have been letting your feelings take the lead. There's a time and a place for that, but the King suggests you may need to exercise a bit more of a firm hand with yourself. Make yourself pay those bills or take that shower, even if you don't *feel* like it, because that's what you need to do to keep the kingdom that is your life running smoothly. Find a way to manage your big feelings enough that you can keep the rest of your life in balance.

Journal Questions for the King of Cups

• There's a good bit going on with the King of Cups if you look for it. Take some time to sit with the imagery on your version of this card and note anything that draws your eye at this moment. What might it be trying to tell you?

• How much are you in control of your emotional state at this moment, and how much is your emotional state in control of you? Sometimes our emotions can get the better of us, and that's completely normal, but it may be time to think about what you can do to get a bit more balance in the mix. Yes, sometimes this means seeking outside help from a therapist or another support resource. A wise King knows when to ask for help.

• Who is in your court? In other words, if you are feeling like you could use some help with the current situation, who can you call upon? If it's hard for you to ask for help, you might also take some time to jot down how you could ask and what that conversation would look like.

• What habits or actions help you feel like the King in this card? When do you feel your most regal, even amidst the chaos of life? How can you bring some of that back into your life at this moment?

• What does it look like when you're feeling in control of your inner state? Consider how you feel in these moments and what's going on around you that contributes to this sense of control.

CHAPTER 39

The suit of wands is most closely associated with the element of fire. They are often depicted as sticks or staffs made of wood, meaning you could burn them to create warmth and light. Wands are the spark of creativity and represent generative powers and making things, whether you're writing a novel or baking an elaborate cake.

Due to their association with fire, the wands are also about passion and enthusiasm. We're not making things on assembly lines here, but rather engaging in craft that fills our soul and enriches our lives. When the wands come up for you, it's a good sign that you should take a moment to *make* something, regardless of whether doing so will earn you any cash or do anything besides fill you with that creative spark that makes life worthwhile.

CHAPTER 40

Begin a New Passion Project with
the Ace of Wands

Ace of Wands

Here we are again at the beginning of another journey through a new Tarot suit. At the start of this journey, we're experiencing a sudden spark of inspiration, an idea essentially handed down to us with divine inspiration.

With the Ace of Wands, we have a single wand, held aloft by a magical hand extended from within a mystical cloud. The wand is very much still connected to the natural world, with its little twigs sprouting small leaves sticking out at various angles. In essence, the hand is offering us this ripe idea, fresh and ready to be transformed as we wish. This is a card that represents that magical feeling of a sudden, brilliant idea that seems almost to come from outside of us by how much its arrival takes us by surprise. The fact that the stick almost seems capable of continuing to grow is a reminder that this card is only the beginning, and we can and should nurture this idea into what it will become.

When the Ace of Wands comes up for you, it's a good time to consider whether you've had any ideas or inspiration recently. Is there something you've been thinking about starting? Some kind of project you've been noodling about for a while, or which you can't get out of your head? The Ace of Wands suggests that now is the time to grab that idea and start trying to make it into something. After all, those verdant leaves won't stay green on this wand forever.

Journal Questions for the Ace of Wands

• What does the wand in this card bring to mind for you? Take a moment to reflect on this image of a lively stick and consider what idea or passion project it may represent in your life at this moment.

• Let's say you already know or have figured out what your big new idea is. What would it take to make it happen? Spend some time brainstorming what steps you'd need to take to move from the idea phase to that of creation and making your project a reality.

• Maybe you've got no idea what this card is talking about, because you haven't been feeling inspired at all recently. This might be a good time to jot down the things you can do to bring that creative spark back to life. What hobbies nurture your soul? When did you had your best ideas in the past?

• Let's find that new idea right now! Set a timer and take some time to just brainstorm new creative projects you can do. This might be writing, art, recipes, or anything else that you enjoy making.

• How do you approach starting something new in your creative life? Do you feel energized by new ideas or overwhelmed at the size of the undertaking? Reflect on your relationship to beginnings and how it has served you in the past.

CHAPTER 41

Decide How to Proceed with the
Two of Wands

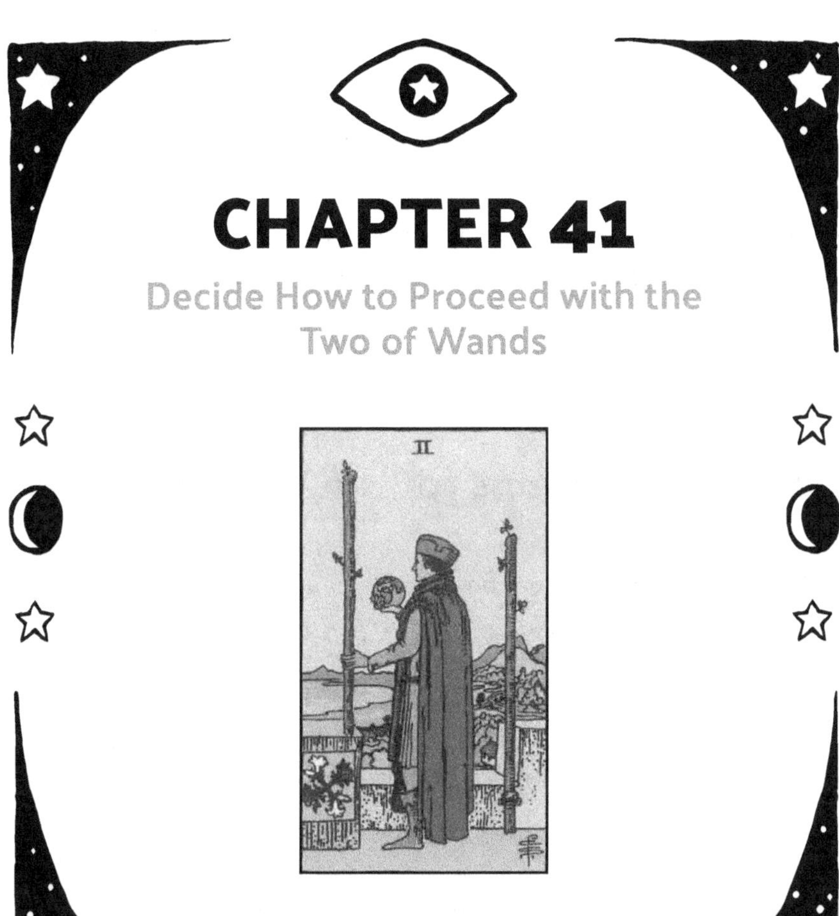

Two of Wands

The twos tend to represent duality and balance, a choice, or a need to bring two seemingly opposing things into alignment. With the wands, we're looking at what it is that you want to create and how you want to move forward. It's a card about planning for the future and making decisions to set yourself up to create whatever it is you're working towards.

In the traditional depiction of the card, we see a man in a cloak standing atop a wall, looking out over the mountains. In one hand, he holds a globe, symbolizing the world of possibilities that lie before him. In the other hand, he clutches a long stick that's being used as a staff—the ideas that his journey rests upon, which he will lean on as he moves forward. Behind him, we see a second staff that's strapped to the wall. We get the sense that perhaps this one will be left behind, a path or idea not taken, not ready to be seized.

When this card comes up, it's time to sit down and make some plans. What do you need to do to move forward with your current goals? What might you need to set aside or leave behind in order to make it happen? While there is much you can achieve, you can't do everything at all once, so you need to choose where your energy goes as you plan ahead.

Journal Questions for the Two of Wands

• Take some time to reflect on the image on your version of the card. What aspects of it are you drawn to, and what might they represent about your current situation?

• What is the "globe" for you right now? If you could dream up anything with the world in the palm of your hands, what would you create in your life?

• Take a moment to consider the skills and tools at your disposal. What do you have already in hand that can help you move forward with your goals?

• Now that you've considered what you already have, what else do you need? How might you get ahold of these additional resources?

• Finally, what might you need to set aside in order to move forward with your current goal? It can be hard to release opportunities or set aside paths that aren't meant for us right now, but sometimes it's necessary. Be honest with yourself here. We can all only take on so much at a time.

CHAPTER 42

Prepare for What Lies Ahead with
the Three of Wands

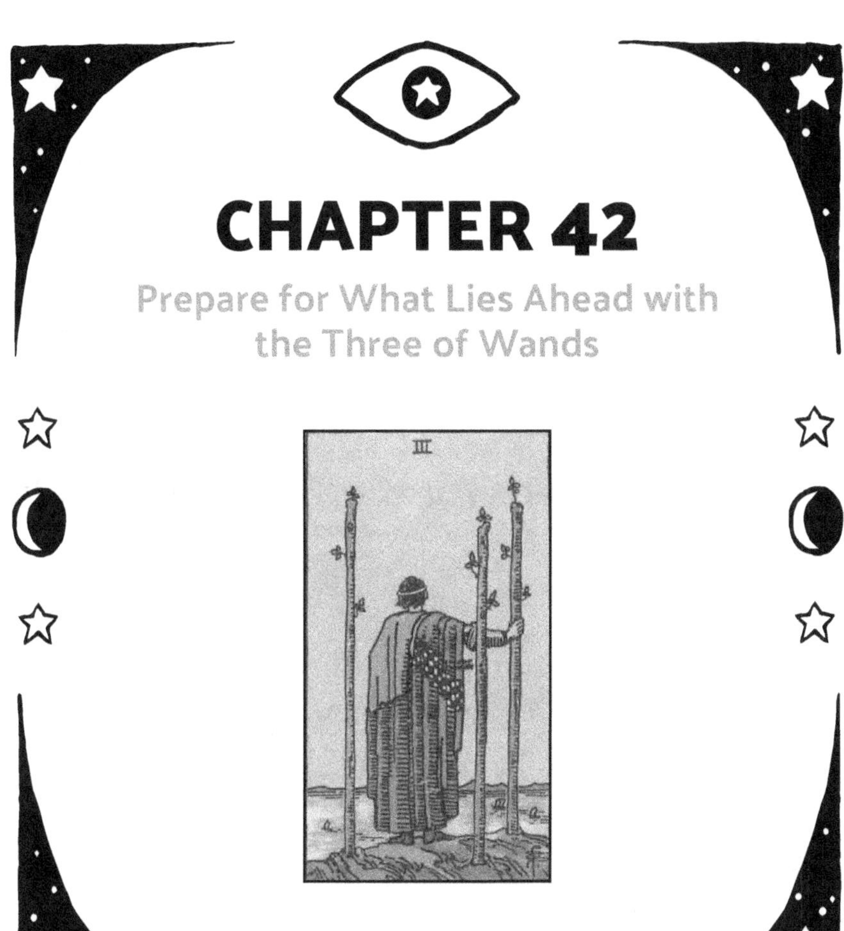

Three of Wands

At first glance, the image of the Three of Wands looks quite similar to the Two. If you ever pulled them back-to-back, it might seem like not too much has happened. But in fact, this card does represent progress on your journey, as much as it also represents preparing for what's to come.

The Three of Wands shows a traveler standing on a rock outcropping overlooking the sea. In the ocean below, three boats float on relatively calm waters. The man holds one staff in his hand, while two others stand upright at his side. Everything about his posture suggests he's preparing for the next leg of his journey, perhaps about to board one of those ships and travel far to grasp his dreams.

The Three of Wands is about looking ahead, about planning for the next leg of the journey. That said, it is also about recognizing how far you've come as you continue to push ahead. Remember, at the Two of Wands, you were about to set out on the journey, looking at the mountains before you. Now, you've crossed them and arrived at the sea where the next leg of your journey awaits. Of course, oversea travel requires a lot of foresight, and you'll need to pause and plan carefully before you continue on your way.

Journal Questions for the Three of Wands

• When you look at your card's depiction of the Three of Wands, what sticks out to you? Why might that be?

• Take a moment to consider your progress so far. When you think of your current goals, what have you accomplished as you work towards them?

• Let's also give some space for past goals already achieved. What have you already accomplished on your journey so far? Congratulate yourself for how far you've come.

• What is the next big step towards creating the life you want? If you were to board a ship and travel to the version of your life that you want to embody, what does that look like?

• What do you want to take with you when you go on this next step of your journey? In other words, what's working well in your life right now that you'd like to continue?

CHAPTER 43

Four of Wands

The Four of Wands as a card just feels like a breath of fresh air, especially after so much careful consideration and preparation in our wands journey thus far. Here, we get to pause and celebrate just how far we've come before pushing on.

In the Rider-Waite depiction, the four wands on this card stand tall, pillars for a celebratory archway from which dangle beautiful flowers and vines. The wands look vibrant and alive, full of that creative energy. Framed between them are two celebrating figures in robes, with floral bouquets held high. This might be a wedding, but the coding is vague enough that it could really be a celebration of just about anything. What we do know is that these figures are full of joy, as are the small background characters further off.

This card is a vibrant moment for celebrating what's been created thus far.

When the Four of Wands shows up for you, it's an invitation to pause and be proud of how far you've come. Too often, we focus on the journey ahead and what's still to come and forget to honor just how much we've already accomplished. The Four of Wands wants you to remember that sometimes it's right and good to just be happy about where you are at this moment. So, pat yourself on the back or throw a little party, even if it's for something relatively small.

Journal Questions for the Four of Wands

• Take a look at your deck's version of the Four of Wands. What parts of the illustration speak to you? What symbols do you resonate with at this moment, and why might that be?

• Take a moment to look back on your journey thus far. What have you achieved? Write a list, and don't take the small stuff for granted. Maybe you didn't paint that beautiful masterpiece, but you did finally go to the art supply store and get the tools you need. Perhaps you haven't worked out every day this week, but you did move your body a little bit more than the week before. Really honor every positive step towards your goals.

• There's plenty to be grateful for outside of our accomplishments. What else can you celebrate in your life at this moment? Yes, this is an invitation to do some gratitude journaling.

• Consider the figures celebrating here and put yourself in their shoes. What is it that you want to celebrate in a month, a week, a year? Use this moment to reflect on all the future goals you want to honor as if they're already accomplished.

• How have you celebrated your achievements in the past? Do you take the time to pat yourself on the back when you accomplish something, or do you already have your eyes on the next goal?

CHAPTER 44

Five of Wands

I won't sugarcoat it—the Five of Wands is some tough energy, but it's part of life and growth. This card is all about conflict and disagreement, about the inherent challenges that come as part of changing and growing. Conflict is never comfortable, but it is often necessary for moving forward.

The Five of Wands shows five figures in a tight, combative huddle. They each wield their wand like a weapon, facing off against one another in whatever disagreement is taking place. Though they're all braced and ready to swing, it doesn't appear any blows have been struck yet here. It's a tense moment, with emotions running high, but it's not gone beyond the point of a more peaceful resolution *quite* yet.

This card often shows up when we're being challenged in some way. Perhaps the people in your life aren't being as supportive of your new goals as you want them to be, or even outright disagree with what you're trying to do. Maybe a coworker has a different approach to a project, one that doesn't fit with how you believe it should be approached. Regardless of whether you've come to metaphorical blows just yet, this card suggests there's some disagreement that needs to be resolved. Sometimes it might mean you need to stop avoiding or pretending this conflict doesn't exist. The simmering resentment of *not* addressing this tension can sometimes be worse than hashing it out in a quick argument that lets all parties speak their minds.

Journal Questions for the Five of Wands

• Look at your card's illustration for the Five of Wands. What stands out about it to you? Do you identify with any of the figures?

• How does it feel to look at this card, and why might that be? Your feelings about this card may well reflect your feelings about conflict, so they're worth exploring.

• Reflect on your approach to conflict for a moment. What is your natural tendency when you encounter disagreement or difference of opinions? How has that approach served you in the past?

• Consider the goal or goals you're currently working towards. Where have you encountered resistance or setbacks?

• If you're in the midst of conflict or a setback right now, take some time to write your way through some possible solutions. How might you resolve the conflict or move forward?

CHAPTER 45

Six of Wands

After the challenges of the Five of Wands, this card is a welcome sight. The Six of Wands is a card of success and accomplishment, of being recognized. Whether you've emerged victorious from the challenges of the Five of Wands or accomplished something else entirely, this is a card about not just celebrating, but being celebrated.

The Six of Wands shows a triumphant and proud figure on horseback. Their posture suggests pride and a sense of self-worth as they hold a staff aloft. At the top of the staff is a wreath, a prize for a victory fairly won. In the background, several other figures walk beside the horseback rider, their wands also held aloft in a signal of celebration. We get the sense that the rider is a figure of honor at this moment, being recognized for their hard work and success.

When the Six of Wands shows up, it's a sign of achievement that's visible for all to see. Perhaps the recognition from others won't come quite the way you expect, but it's likely that you'll feel in some way celebrated for what you've accomplished recently. Maybe it's a promotion at work or maybe just a bit of praise from a colleague. Be open to receiving the rewards, large and small, for what you've accomplished thus far. And if they don't seem forthcoming, take matters into your own hands and celebrate yourself a little. Share that accomplishment loudly and be proud for the world to see.

Journal Questions for the Six of Wands

• What speaks to you in your version of the Six of Wands? Do you see yourself in the figure being celebrated or the celebrants?

• How have you been recognized for your accomplishments in the past? Consider how you prefer to be seen or not seen for what you've done. Does the attention make you uncomfortable, or does it spur you on?

• What have you achieved that you deserve to be recognized for? Write your accomplishments out and consider if there are ways you can share them to ensure others appreciate how far you've come.

• If being acknowledged by others isn't your style, how might you reward yourself? Think through the ways you can treat yourself or recognize your own accomplishments that will feel celebratory and nourishing.

• It's important to recognize and celebrate our community as well. How do you celebrate others in your life when they accomplish something?

CHAPTER 46

Seven of Wands

The Seven of Wands reminds us of the importance of sticking true to our goals even in the face of adversity. In a single word, this card says "persevere." It won't always be easy, but you're on the right path and it's time to stand your ground even when you meet setbacks.

In the Rider-Waite depiction, we see a single figure holding a staff across their body in a defensive posture. They have the high ground here, standing above the menacing staves in the foreground. Clearly, they're bracing themselves for an attack, but they're in the better position here. No matter that others are against them—they're in the right, and they're ready to stand their ground.

When the Seven of Wands shows up, it may signify a challenge to come, or one that you're currently facing. This card is a message that setbacks shouldn't mean you give up or stop trying. Rather, if you know you're on the right path, these challenges are merely roadblocks which you can and should push through. It can be a scary card to see at first, but really the message is a positive one—keep going, don't mind the stumbling blocks, you've got this.

Journal Questions for the Seven of Wands

• Reflect on your card's image for the Seven of Wands. What sticks out to you or draws your eye? What might that represent for you in this moment?

• Consider the defensive position of the figure on the card. Where in your life do you feel you are in defense mode right now? Consider whether you're tensing against an imagined challenge or a real one, and whether this is a position you should continue to defend.

• If this is a real challenge, consider your position and that of the other party or parties. Jot down your perspective and the other perspective, and take some time to consider if they can be brought into alignment. How can you resolve this conflict without a battle?

• What does defense mode look like for you? When you're feeling attacked, how do you respond? How has that worked out in the past?

• What challenges have you faced in the past that you were able to overcome? Sometimes, it's helpful to write down some of the things we've managed to get through in the past as a way of reminding ourselves that we are strong and can move through some pretty tough things

CHAPTER 47

Seize Forward Momentum with
the Eight of Wands

Eight of Wands

The Eight of Wands is a card that just shouts movement and forward momentum. When you pull this card, it's a sign that you're on the right path, and you should keep moving full steam ahead.

The imagery of the Eight of Wands is relatively straightforward, featuring no human figures and not much detail in the background. The majority of the image is taken up by eight staves with little leaves indicating growth. The staffs are shown at a slant, and we get the sense that they're racing forward, in constant motion. Behind them is a gently rolling field with a river flowing through it, showing that things are relatively calm and still aside from the sticks themselves.

This card suggests things may begin to move quickly now. If

you've been working to achieve something, you might suddenly start to see more forward momentum. If you've been considering taking a leap, this card may well be saying "Jump, now! The time is right!" Where so many Tarot cards invite reflection, this isn't one of them. This is a card of quick, decisive action.

Journal Questions for the Eight of Wands

• What does the image of these fast-paced staffs moving through space evoke for you? Spend some time reflecting on the image of your version of this card and what it brings up.

• Where in your life have you been hesitating to take action? Is there a good reason for this hesitation, or is it just you holding yourself back?

• Are you someone who can easily take swift, decisive action? Or do you tend to weigh your options and second-guess things? This card is a reminder that there's a time and place for each approach, and it's helpful to know which one you tend to lean into.

• If you could snap your fingers and make something happen in your life, what would it be? What steps can you take to move quickly towards making this a reality, right now?

• Can you think of a time when you delayed action and wish you hadn't? Are there opportunities you could have seized, but didn't? What can you learn from these past moments to help you identify when moving swiftly towards something might be a good idea in the future?

CHAPTER 48

Nine of Wands

All that forward motion from the Eight of Wands was necessary, but it likely also left you a bit exhausted. The Nine of Wands is a much-needed pause after so much hard work.

In the Rider-Waite depiction, the Nine of Wands shows a figure leaning on their staff. The figure stands in front of eight sticks, which almost look like a forest. There is a sense of weary pause about this card, showing that the figure has stopped to gather their strength before moving on. They've clearly been through a lot, but quite literally not out of the woods yet. This moment of respite is a necessary one, but the journey isn't over, and there's more to be done before the final goal is achieved.

The Nine of Wands may not look it at first glance, but it's a positive card. Sure, you've been through a lot, and sure, you're not quite at the end of the road yet, but we're at card nine out of ten here! Your final goal is so close, and you've just got to gather your strength to work for a bit longer before you hit that sense of accomplishment. Then you can truly rest on your laurels for a bit before we begin again at step 1.

Journal Questions for the Nine of Wands

• What comes to mind when you look at your version of the Nine of Wands? Do you relate to the tired figure or are you more drawn to the wands in the background? Why might that be?

• If you're feeling that weariness we see in the Nine of Wands, take a moment to ask yourself how you spend your time resting. This may seem like a strange question, but often we get so caught up in the day-to-day that we forget what true rest and self-care should look like for us. What can you do to refill your energy reserves right now?

• There may be four wands ahead of the figure, but there are three behind them. What are these three wands for you? In other words, reflect on what you've accomplished and what you've been working on that has you feeling so tired. It took a lot of energy, but you did achieve something, and it's important to acknowledge that.

• Now let's look at the wands that lie ahead. What do you still need to check off your to-do list before you can consider your current mission accomplished? Make an old-fashioned to-do list and make it as actionable as possible.

• Look at the staff our figure is leaning on. This is a representation of our support system, the people and resources we can lean on. Who and/or what in your life can support you as you take a necessary break before you continue?

CHAPTER 49

Ten of Wands

As far as the tens go, the Ten of Wands doesn't exactly scream celebration, but it's a moment of accomplishment, nevertheless. Did we maybe take on too much in our rush to achieve? Yes. But it's not forever, and we've got what it takes to carry this weight.

The Ten of Wands shows a figure clearly struggling to carry the bundle of ten wands that he's been tasked to carry. He's bent over, bracing himself as he tries to keep all ten of these staffs in order. There's a sense of forward momentum, but it seems a bit on the slow side, like if he could lay down one or two of these sticks, he might reach the town in the distance a bit more quickly.

When I pull the Ten of Wands, I see it as an invitation to consider what responsibilities I can set aside. The completion aspect of this Ten of Wands is a bit of a "girl bossed too hard" kind of vibe, where your hard work earned you so many wonderful new opportunities that you may have taken on a bit too much. It's great that you got here, but you also can't *stay* here for too long. You can't carry all these sticks forever, and you may already be feeling a bit exhausted from trying. This card reminds us that we don't have to take on all the responsibilities all at once, and we need to prioritize and pare back a bit to what is most essential at this moment.

Journal Questions for the Ten of Wands

• What do you feel when you look at your version of the Ten of Wands? What emotions or past memories come up? Give these topics some space and write about them.

• So, what are you carrying right now? Make a list of all the things you're juggling that feel essential.

• What can you let go? You don't have to say no to that new opportunity forever, but maybe it needs a "not right now." Think about what you can lay aside so you can focus on the most important things without burning out.

• Who or what can help you carry this burden? Look at your list of "essential" to-dos and responsibilities. Are you able to get support in these areas? Maybe you can set the bills to autopay so that's one less task per month, or maybe there's a friend or partner you can lean on a bit more for some support.

• Remember how this card is a *ten*, a sense of accomplishment or completion? Take a moment to reflect on what led you to carry all these darn sticks. I'm betting some of them were things you really wished for and wanted, whether it's the responsibility of caring for a child or pet, or the tasks that come with your dream job.

Court Cards and the Wands

With the ten-card journey complete, we've reached the Court Cards in the suit of Wands. Here, we see different reflections of creativity and creation as we walk through the phases of Page, Knight, Queen, and King. Each member of the court of Wands has a different lesson to share and a different aspect of the wand's fiery energy for us.

CHAPTER 50

Create from a Beginner's Mind
with the Page of Wands

Page of Wands

As a writer, the Page of Wands is one of my absolute favorite cards to pull. This card is all about the fresh start feeling of having a new idea or project, or about that moment when your enthusiasm feels brand new even if you've been working on something for a while.

The Page of Wands features a chipper young figure who's proudly holding on to their staff. They are dressed to the nines, ready to embark on a journey in their traveling boots, hat, and cloak. In the distance, there are mountains ahead and a path below their feet. This is someone at the start of a journey, and they are thrilled about what's to come.

When you pull the Page of Wands, it often suggests you've entered or will soon be stepping into a time of inspiration and creative energy. Maybe you just had a new idea or found the time to try a hobby that you've always wanted to get into. On the other hand, it's possible the Page showed up because you're not feeling that inspired enthusiasm at all. This card can also be an invitation to step back into the beginner's mindset and try to recapture the spark you felt at the start of a journey or project. Sometimes, that creative fire comes naturally and other times, we need to spend a little time tending to it to keep it burning.

Journal Questions for the Page of Wands

• Take some time looking at the imagery of this card. What aspects are you drawn to? Do you resonate with the figure's energetic stance, or do you find yourself drawn to the challenging mountains in the distance?

• When did you last feel that Page of Wands excitement about something? Take a moment to consider your creative life and when it last felt charged with potential.

• Maybe you're feeling the creative spark right now! If so, jot down your idea and spend some time brainstorming how you can make it a reality.

• If you're in the middle of a project, maybe it's time to recapture the Page of Wands mentality. Write about what inspired you to begin this project or creation. How can you look at your work from a fresh angle to make it feel new and exciting all over again?

• You've got a journey ahead, and it's great that you're so excited right now. But what do you need to hold on to as you start your quest? What do you need to have access to keep going on the new idea or project you're working on, or to refresh your energy after it wanes?

CHAPTER 51

Knight of Wands

Knights bring the "full speed ahead" energy to their suits; in the case of the Knight of Wands, that means taking all that creative energy and putting it towards making something. Making *the* thing, ideally, whatever it is that fills you with passion and the need to create.

The Knight of Wands is depicted atop his horse, and they're both moving full speed ahead. The horse's hooves are high in the air, as if it is positively bounding towards the goal. The Knight's tunic blows back in the wind from their hasty march towards their goal. He holds the wand aloft, more a steady and stable presence than a weapon in this moment. It is a tool, the mark of the creative energy he is bringing with him as he takes on this latest quest.

When I pull the Knight of Wands, the message is clear: "stop dreaming, start doing." You've got the creative potential, the ideas, and the excitement, all built up, but it doesn't mean much unless you apply it to something. This card is a sign that it's time to stop planning your project and actually pick up the paint brush, put your fingers to the keyboard, or buy the ingredients for that new recipe. Whatever it is you've been dreaming of making, the Knight of Wands asks what you're waiting for. Go make the thing.

Journal Questions for the Knight of Wands

• When you look at your card's image, where do you see yourself? Are you the eager horse, carrying its rider to the goal? Perhaps you're the Wand, the figure through which creative potential is challenged. Wherever you see yourself in your version of this card, take some time to reflect on what that may mean for where you are right now.

• Well, what is it? What's that burning idea, the passion project, the thing you've been thinking about but haven't yet put into motion? Spend some time putting those ideas down on paper so you can move from ideation to creation.

• Consider the horse in this card. Who or what can help carry you towards your goal and support you in making this dream a reality?

• Now let's think about the wand. What tools do you have to help you build what you've been envisioning? What tools do you still need to realistically begin?

• So what should you do if you're unsure about the action this card is inviting you to take? Take some time to consider the last time you had a big idea or passion, something you wanted to do or make. Write down anything that comes to mind, then ask yourself—what do I want to bring into being?

CHAPTER 52

Nurture Your Capabilities with the Queen of Wands

Queen of Wands

The Queen of Wands is a calmer, more steady creation energy. Whereas the Page is all about vibrant fresh ideas, the Queen of Wands is about honoring your creative abilities and inspiring others to do the same.

In the Rider-Waite depiction, the Queen of Wands sits on her throne in a self-assured stance. Her legs are spread and she sits tall, taking up as much space as possible. This is someone who is confident in their abilities and aims to inspire others to believe in what they can do, too. In her right hand, she holds a staff which represents the creative Wand energy of this card. In her left hand, she holds a blooming flower, a further reminder that she is full of fertile energy, which creates and sustains. At her feet rests a cat, a nod to the Queen's ability to care for and support other beings even as she channels her own generative powers. In the background, we see planes on one side and mountains on the other. She bridges the gap between these worlds, bringing together disparate energies and maintaining them in a state of calm creation.

The Queen of Wands is a card that essentially says, "you got this." It's a reminder to own your abilities, that confidence can go a long way, and that you've earned the right to yours. The Queen does not apologize for taking up space with her ideas, and neither should you. At the same time, the nurturing energy of this card gently suggests that you may benefit from getting others involved in a team effort here, inspiring those around you to pitch in to accomplish the goal.

Journal Questions for the Queen of Wands

• There's a lot of imagery to choose from in this card. Take some time to reflect on your deck's depiction of the Queen of Wands. Which images draw your attention, and why?

• Consider the Queen's firm but gentle posture of confidence. Where in your life do you find it relatively natural to embody this space of quiet confidence in your abilities? Where is it challenging?

• The Queen is surrounded by blooming flowers in this card. What do you bring to life or aspire to bring to life? How can you use your strengths to further these goals?

• Let's look at the disparate background for a moment. Are there areas of your life that feel in opposition right now? Perhaps you're struggling with work/life balance or feel torn between your family of origin and other relationships in your life. Take some time to reflect on how you might be able to help better bridge these gaps in your life, or accept them as they are, if that is what you're called to do.

• Who around can you recruit for Team You? As you think about the projects or goals you're trying to bring into existence, where might you be able to inspire others to help out or pitch in with skills that you yourself might lack?

CHAPTER 53

Look to the Long Game with the King of Wands

King of Wands

The King of Wands is steadfast in his abilities, like the Queen, but he takes on a leadership and planning role when it comes to bringing things into being. Where the Queen gently inspires, the King commands. He has looked ahead, made the plan, and he's going to act on it to bring his vision into being.

The King of Wands is shown from the side rather than directly facing us like the Queen. It gives him a bit of distance, a sense of looking out over the horizon rather than at us, his subjects. This far-off look shows just how much time the King of Wands spends planning ahead, taking all that creative Wands energy, and making a step-by-step list of how to bring it to fruition. The King holds his staff out in front of him in a firm, straight line, a further symbol of how the King of Wands holds true to his ideals and is always one step ahead of the rest. He knows where he's going, and he isn't going to budge once he's decided how to get there. A small lizard-like creature sits at his side; a salamander further representing the fiery energy inherent in this card.

When the King of Wands pops up, it's time to make a plan. Whereas the Knight rushes forward to bring things into being, the King is the one who told him to go there and do that. This card suggests the need to ground into your intention and spend some time envisioning how you will bring that creative energy toward your project or goal. It's a "sit down, plan it out, and then tell someone to do it" kind of card, bringing big management energy to the table. Even if you're a team of one. However, you might need to use leadership skills on yourself to get things moving when this card comes up.

Journal Questions for the King of Wands

• Take a look at your version of this card. What stands out to you? Do you relate to the King in his standoffish confidence? Perhaps you're the salamander, small but full of fire.

• Are you a planner or a bit of a seat-of-your-pants kind of person when it comes to your goals and creative life? Consider your habits and patterns, and how they've served you in the past.

• Make a plan! Take the time to consider the concrete steps and actions that you need to take in order to bring your passion project or goal to life. Look ahead here, anticipating what you'll need in the future, not just right in this moment.

• Are you a leader or a follower? Consider how you can channel the leadership energy of the King to support your goals in life right now. This may not mean going around telling others what to do, but it might involve some firm conversations with yourself.

• Consider the last time you felt "in charge" when it comes to your creative life. Do you tend to let creativity come to you, or are there ways that you can cultivate new ideas and energy around goals?

CHAPTER 54

Bring Thoughts into Action
with the Swords

I won't lie to you; the suit of swords can seem like a bit of a tough hang when you first look at them. They're sharp edges, swift, and occasionally scary. But the swords are about forward progress, and sometimes you have to do away with what's no longer serving you in order to move forward. Swords are linked to the element of air, so they're closely connected with our thoughts and our words. They may seem sharp and cutting, but often this is a metaphor for the way our own anxieties and fears get in the way. The swords unite thought with action, a reminder that what we think, we become.

CHAPTER 55

Break Through to What's New with the Ace of Swords

Ace of Swords

The Ace of Swords begins our journey through the suit with the sharp, sudden arrival of a new idea or way of doing things. Picture it cutting right through those stale old patterns to reveal something new and exciting underneath.

The Ace of Swords shows a hand bursting forth from a cloud, holding a single sword aloft. The blade is pointed straight up towards the heavens, slicing right towards higher-minded ideas and ways of approaching things. Atop the sword, a crown rests perfectly balanced, suggesting that this new breakthrough may well lead to a moment of glorious achievement. Plants burst forth from the crown, further illustrating this as a time of growth.

When I see this card, it's like a more sharp-edged version of that new spark feeling from the Ace of Wands. Whereas the Wands are about creative energy and creative spark, I see the Swords as a bit more cutting than that. It's a new idea, yes, but it's likely to be one that cuts through or breaks with what you thought you knew. It's swift, it's sudden, and it doesn't take no for an answer—this is a change that demands attention *right now.*

Journal Questions for the Ace of Swords

• What draws your attention to your version of this card? What might those images have to say about what's happening in your life right now?

• What is the sword for you? Is there something that's just begging for a shift, a change, a new approach in your life?

• Let's take a moment to focus on that mysterious hand bursting forth from the cloud. Consider it your source of inspiration, the guiding force that pushes you to be better. What is this force for you? In other words, what is your "why" for that which you're seeking to change in your life right now?

• What would it look like to wear the crown that's balanced on this sword? In other words, where are you trying to go in life at this moment? When will you consider your current goal or goals accomplished?

• Much like those mysterious plants blooming from inside the crown, you need nourishment to keep growing. Take some time to reflect on what you can do to fuel your journey even as you implement this new idea or change.

CHAPTER 56

Make the Tough Choice with the Two of Swords

Two of Swords

Once upon a time, I pulled the Two of Swords *constantly*. This card is about indecision, feeling stuck between two options to the point where you just... do nothing. For me, it came up because I was stuck between the financial stability of my day job and the unknown of leaving it to pursue my dreams. I couldn't decide which path to choose, so I just stayed stuck. Fast forward to now, when the card has absented itself from the deck I'm using as I write this book entirely. It doesn't want to be found, and I guess it's because I chose my path, that years-long question finally answered.

The Two of Swords, in the Rider-Waite depiction, features a woman sitting on a stone bench. She wears a blindfold, suggesting she is willfully avoiding making a choice here. In her crossed arms, she holds two swords, making an X in front of her body with them.

The moon shines in a crescent sliver in the background, a reminder of the way we can hide things from ourselves and rely on illusions instead. She is stuck between these two choices, two swords, but she could see a path forward if only she'd lay them down a moment, take off the blindfold, and allow herself to see clearly.

When the Two of Swords comes up, it's a bit of a wake-up call. This card says, hey, why are you avoiding making a decision? What are you refusing to see or blocking yourself from choosing the path forward? When I see the Two of Swords, it's time for a good hard look at what I've been avoiding, which isn't always fun, but is necessary if you want to get unstuck

Journal Questions for the Two of Swords

• There's plenty to look at here, so let's take a moment to reflect on the imagery of this card. What draws your attention, and why might that be?

• Consider the blindfold. What do you reach for when you're trying to numb out or avoid thinking about something? How has this served you in the past?

• What are the swords for you right now? Are there two options or paths you're trying to choose between, even if you've been resistant to admitting it? Write down these two (or more!) directions your life could go and spend some time imagining what it might look like to choose that choice.

• Are there feelings you've been trying to avoid? As much as this card is about thinking things through, it's also about letting yourself be open to your heart. Consider if it's an emotional block that's preventing you from taking off the blindfold to find the path forward.

• We've envisioned our future paths and where they diverge, and we've looked at the emotions surrounding them. Now, choose a path forward. Reflect on what it would take to follow that path, to make that choice. What would you need to have, to do, to be, in order to make it happen?

CHAPTER 57

Three of Swords

Whenever I pull the Three of Swords, I confess my initial reaction is to wince. This card just *looks* painful, with the three swords puncturing a heart front and center. Like any card in Tarot, however, it isn't all bad. In fact, some of our biggest growth moments and most important lessons come from those punch-in-the-gut Three of Swords periods of life.

The Three of Swords shows a Hallmark-style heart being pierced by three swords, which crisscross their way through it and out to the other side. There are rain clouds in the background and a torrential downpour. The entire image just screams "you're having a bad time." The rain and heart are a reminder that you're probably feeling tender and emotional about whatever is going on right now.

The Three of Swords is grief. It's sorrow; it's heartbreak; it's all those big hard emotions we must travel through in life. When I pull this card, I feel profound compassion for the past versions of myself who sat long and hard in these difficult moments. I feel scared for my future self, because life will always bring another Three of Swords just as sure as you'll see another celebratory 10 of Cups. This card is an invitation to be gentle with yourself. If you're in the middle of these big feelings, navigating grief and sorrow and heartbreak, you don't have to shake it off right away. Let yourself feel those feelings, or you'll stay pinned down by them like the heart is pinned by the swords.

This card is also a gentle reminder that even though they're tough, these moments of emotional turmoil are often the ones that help us grow. Maybe not right now, in this exact moment when you're going through it, but one day you'll probably look back and see how much you learned from overcoming this hard time right here.

Journal Questions for the Three of Swords

• What does the image of this card bring up for you? Do you immediately relate to that "swords-through-the-heart" feeling? What about the rain clouds?

• If you're in the Three of Swords right now, big time, take this as an invitation to just... rest. Write down some of your favorite ways to rest and restore. Then go do them.

• When you're ready, take a moment to look back on some of the hard times you've had in the past. What did they teach you or give you? Did you come out stronger? Did you learn something?

• What is going on for you right now that feels like the Three of Swords? Let the feelings out. Write down all the reasons and the ways you feel hurt and heartbroken right now. If this is really challenging to do on your own, I recommend working with a therapist who specializes in grief.

• What can you learn from this hard thing right now? If you're in the right space, take some time to look ahead and consider where you might find the silver lining in this difficult moment.

CHAPTER 58

Four of Swords

After all the pain of the Three of Swords, is it any wonder that the Four invites us to rest and recover? The Four of Swords is a card of repose, of resting and restoring our energy before we carry on.

In the traditional depiction, the Four of Swords shows a knight in full armor. He is lying upon a slab that, frankly, doesn't look very comfortable—in fact, it looks an awful lot like a tomb. His hands are crossed over his body, a pose of rest and contemplation. Three swords hang from the wall behind the Knight, while the fourth lies resting at his side. The swords on the wall represent past accomplishments, trophies of dragons slain, and villages saved. But the one on the floor beside the Knight suggests he isn't finished, just taking a pause before heading back out for the next adventure.

A stained-glass window in the background suggests his locale is a church or place of worship, and perhaps this moment of rest is also a time to check in for guidance and spiritual support.

When the Four of Swords comes up, it means it's time to rest right now. The card's association with a tomb is a reminder that we all need rest, that we can't keep going without restoring our energy or else we'll face burnout or worse. The Four of Swords says, "you've done plenty, but it's taken plenty out of you." Take time to check in with yourself and your higher power if you believe in one. Pause, reflect, and fill your cup before you even think about picking up that sword to get back out into the fray.

Journal Questions for the Four of Swords

• This is a card that's ripe with images. Spend some time reflecting on your version of this card and which elements stick out to you. What might they be trying to say?

• What does rest mean for you? Are you resistant to resting and if so, why might that be?

• Take a moment to reflect on the stained-glass window here. What is your guiding light, the higher meaning that keeps you going? This might be a spiritual or religious thing, or it may be a belief or goal. When you're checking in with the bigger picture, what do you connect to?

• The swords on the wall are trophies, but they also point towards the knight, a danger should they fall. What are the risks if you just keep collecting accomplishments without rest? Has there been a time in your life when you've overdone it like this? How did that go for you?

• Take some time to contemplate your next move before you move forward. This card doesn't just invite us to rest but to plan ahead. What is next for you in the journey of life? What are you trying to accomplish when you pick up that sword and head back out into the world?

CHAPTER 59

Five of Swords

The Five of Swords is another tough one, carrying on with the Swords theme of hard-won lessons and growth. It's a card about conflict and competition, but also a warning about the risks of putting your desire to win above your relationships.

In the Five of Swords, a figure in the foreground looks over their shoulder while picking up swords from the beach. They're holding two of them with a third in their hand, and we get the sense they'll keep collecting until all five are in their grasp. The figure looks content in his moment of victory collecting the swords, and perhaps it is, in a way. But in the background, two distraught figures walk away. One appears to be in tears while the other simply slumps off. These are the people who lost their swords, and they're leaving the victor behind. The sword collector may have won, but there's a real cost to this victory, a sense that the relationships have been severed, that the prize has come at too high a cost.

If you pull the Five of Swords, it's time to get clear on what's important. If there's a conflict or difficult situation, you need to tread carefully and weigh your options. Is coming out on top really the goal here, or are there relationships that matter more to you than winning ever could? This card warns you to really think through the consequences before you run in, blade swinging, to take the prize.

Journal Questions for the Five of Swords

• When you look at the imagery on this card, what stands out to you? Why might that be?

• Are you in a situation of conflict or disagreement right now? If so, what would "winning" mean to you? What would it take to get there?

• Consider the other people involved in the conflict. If you win, what do they stand to lose? Can you get what you want without doing lasting damage to the relationships here, or is there another approach you need to take?

• When faced with conflict, which of the figures in this card do you tend to be? Are you the one who stays behind, winning at all costs, collecting the spoils after the battle ends? Or do you give in too easily, becoming the ones who walk away in defeat?

• There's a time and a place for both approaches depending on what you ultimately want to prioritize. Consider the situation at hand and what truly matters to you long term. How might you move forward and keep hold of the most important things?

CHAPTER 60

Six of Swords

The Six of Swords is bittersweet, and I always have mixed feelings when it comes up for me. This is a card about progress, but it's also about the necessity of leaving some things behind in order to grow and move on to the next stage. When I see this card, I always think of a time in my life when everything I'd known was coming to an end all at once. In the span of a month, I left my job, moved to a new state, and started a new graduate program. These were all necessary changes for the next stage of my life, but there was so much I felt sad to leave behind. That's what the Six of Swords means to me—the excitement of the next leg of the journey, coupled with the sorrow of what you leave behind to pursue it.

In the Six of Swords, we see a figure in a boat, hunched over as they use a pole to push ahead. The figure's posture suggests a sense of loss, and their back is facing toward us, furthering the idea that they're leaving something behind. The boat has several sacks that look full of supplies, and there are six swords standing at the ready. The figure has everything they need for the journey ahead, and it's a green shore they're paddling towards. They are ready for this journey, and it's ultimately a path towards something good. But first, for a moment, there are things from the past that they need to let go of before they embrace the change that lies ahead.

When you see the Six of Swords, it's a reminder that change is both inevitable and necessary. That, yes, sometimes transitions are hard, but they're often worth it in the end. You have everything you need to make this leap, to transform in ways that life is calling you to. It's okay to take a moment to acknowledge what you're leaving behind, but then, my friend, you need to push on and keep that boat moving forward.

Journal Questions for the Six of Swords

• When you look at this card, what do you see? What draws your attention, and why?

• Are you staring down a big change or transition in life right now? If so, take this moment to reflect on and honor that which will get left behind in the process.

• If you're not looking at a big transition at this moment, reflect on a previous one. How did you feel before, during, and after the change? What did you leave behind, and what did you gain?

• If you're getting ready to embark on a change, take a moment to take stock. What's in your boat? What supplies and support do you have on this journey? Is there anything else that you need?

• What will you gain from letting this change come through your life? Where are you headed, and what do you have to look forward to when you get there?

CHAPTER 61

Get Away with Something with the Seven of Swords

Seven of Swords

I just love the sneakiness of the Seven of Swords. We all keep secrets sometimes, and this card just unabashedly embraces the fact that every now again, a bit of stealth is a strategic move. That's not to say we shouldn't use caution and our best judgement if we are trying to slip under the radar; this card can also come up when we're experiencing imposter syndrome and *feel* like we're getting away with something, even when we're not. If I pulled a card every day during my first week of grad school, I swear I'd have seen the Seven of Swords each time, because I was convinced they had accepted me by accident.

The Seven of Swords shows a figure sneaking away from a camp, holding five swords cradled in his arms, blade first. Frankly, a risky move to hold the swords towards himself in this way, which is a reminder that we always risk a bit of a cut if we try to be a bit loose with the truth or outright deceive someone. Even so, the figure looks pleased with himself even as he's looking over his shoulder to make sure he doesn't get caught, making off with five of the camp's seven precious swords. At this moment in time, anyway, it looks like he's going to get away with it and make off safely with his bounty.

This card is a complex one, as its meaning can truly vary depending on what's going on for you at the time when you draw it. This card can mean that deception is afoot—either your own or someone else's. It may well be an invitation to examine your relationship with the truth and take stock of how you've been acting lately. However, the Seven of Wands can also be a sign of acting strategically. Sometimes, we need to take a vacation day even if we don't plan to do anything but rest. It may *feel* like getting away with something, but really, it's just a carefully considered use of your resources. When the Seven of Wands comes up, be honest with yourself—are you getting away with something that may not be in your best interest long-term, or are you acting strategically to best serve your goals?

Journal Questions for the
Seven of Swords

• Where in this card do you see yourself right now? Are you the figure sneaking off, or the camp that's being robbed without their knowledge?

• Is there a time in your life when you felt like you were getting away with something? Upon reflection, were you actually tricking everyone, or was it imposter syndrome in action?

• What is your relationship to openness and honesty? Do you walk through life as an open book, or do you prefer to keep your secrets tucked close to your chest? How has this served you?

• Consider whether there are places in your life where careful, strategic action may be called for. Is there an area where you may need to tread cautiously and perhaps even a bit sneakily to get what you want or need?

• Let's say you are sneaking off with a handful of swords, like this card suggests. What are those swords? In other words, is there something you feel like you have to be crafty to get? Think about affection from others and your needs. Are they being met easily and openly?

CHAPTER 62

Process Your Negative Thoughts with the Eight of Swords

Eight of Swords

If anxiety had a mascot, it'd be the Eight of Swords. This card is all about the ways in which our own thoughts can make us feel trapped, even when we could escape at any time. It's a card that's near and dear to me as someone who's had anxiety since the moment I gained consciousness. Even though this card embodies anxiety, I see it as a positive one because it reminds us of that old saying, "what we think, we become." We have the power to recognize our anxious thoughts and challenge them, and this card is an invitation to do so.

The Eight of Swords shows a woman standing in an open desert, surrounded by swords. She is bound and blindfolded, and at first glance, it looks like she's in a sticky situation. However, a closer look reveals that the gaps in the swords are quite wide enough for her to pass through. She isn't truly surrounded. Her bindings are quite loose, as well, and she could very easily slip them off if she tried. But here she stays, letting herself be trapped because she believes that she is. She can't see the ease with which she might escape because she hasn't let herself consider it.

When you pull the Eight of Swords, take a good hard look at where you're feeling stuck. Then, ask yourself if you're being honest about how impossible the situation seems. Chances are, if the Eight of Swords has come knocking, you're largely trapped by your own thoughts and perceptions, not by the reality of the situation. That doesn't mean what you're going through isn't difficult. However, you might see a way forward if you let yourself shake free of those loose bonds and see the gaps between the swords that currently feel like a prison.

Journal Questions for the Eight of Swords

• What stands out to you when you look at this card? What feelings or memories do the images evoke?

• Are you feeling stuck right now? Take some time to jot down where you're feeling trapped or like you're in a bit of a stalemate.

• Now, consider the reality of those situations you listed out. Take some time to brainstorm a path forward, a way out. What might you not be seeing because you're stuck in the idea that you're stuck?

• What are the ties that bind you? When you think of your mental patterns and habits, where do you most often become anxious or feel like you can't get out of a situation? In other words, what holds you back or sends you spiraling into a bad mood?

• You are stronger than you think, and you can slip right out of your current mental bind. To help remember this fact, write out previous moments in life where you felt trapped or a bit hopeless. Did you overcome them? Was it as hard as you thought?

CHAPTER 63

Acknowledge Your Fears with the Nine of Swords

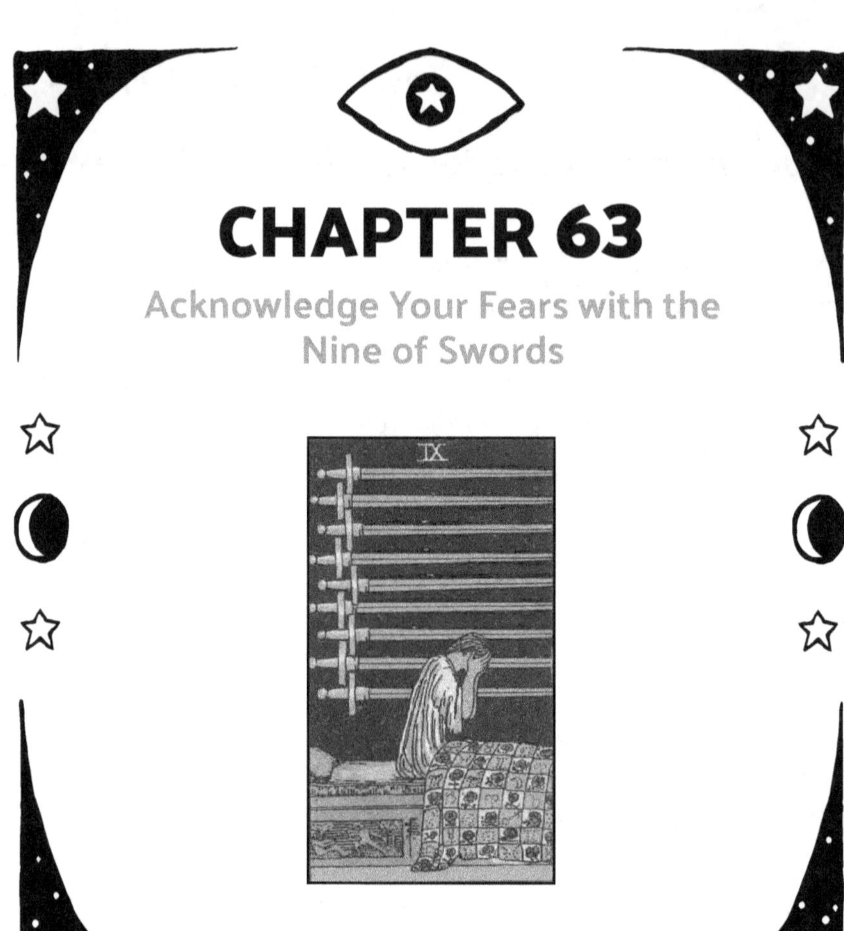

Nine of Swords

Where the Eight of Swords shows your self-limiting tendencies, the Nine of Swords reflects how all-consuming worry and fear can become. This card is what happens when you're afraid, depressed, or otherwise navigating difficult thoughts and feelings that leave you feeling exhausted and, yes, a bit trapped.

The Nine of Swords shows a figure sitting up in bed, their face in their hands. We get the sense they've just woken from a terrible dream or nightmare, or perhaps they're so overcome with grief or worry that they can't fall asleep at all. On the wall, swords are lined up in neat rows, like worries collected and tended to so often that they're basically a decoration at this point. This person has been collecting their fears and worries, keeping them close even at bedtime when they ought to rest. It's no surprise they're having trouble sleeping.

When the Nine of Swords shows up, it's likely you're having a tough time, and you've been in this place for a while. Fears or worries may be taking their toll on you right now, robbing you of the sleep and rest that you need to function. It's not a place you ever want to be, and yet, it's a part of life. This card's message is that you have to stop giving your fears so much power. Stop hanging them up in the bedroom like honored guests. Give yourself time to process and acknowledge your fears, but don't let them own you

Journal Questions for the Nine of Swords

• What aspects of this card draw your attention, and why might that be?

• Is something keeping you up at night? Take some time to write down those worries and fears, putting them on paper so they can stop floating around in your head.

• If you're in a space to do so, dig a little deeper with those worries and fears. How likely are they to come to pass, really? Would it be as bad as you think if they did? Do take care here, and work with a therapist or mental health professional if this is difficult for you.

• What are your swords? In other words, do you have worries and fears that you come back to time and time again, so much so that they're practically polished in a place of honor on the list of things that keep you up at night?

• Look at the list of common fears and worries that you come back to. Is there a common theme or underlying reason that these particular anxieties come back to you again and again? Flip those fears around and consider what they say about your values. For instance, if you constantly worry about something bad happening to a loved one, you might practice gratitude for having such a cherished relationship(s) in your life.

CHAPTER 64

Honor Your Pain with the Ten of Swords

Ten of Swords

Whenever I see the Ten of Swords, my first instinct is just to say "ouch!" This card looks painful, and it often comes up for us during or just before a painful period of our life. The good news is, even though it may hurt, it's a ten. It's the end of something, not the beginning. Ripping off the bandage is painful, but once it's done, it's done.

The Ten of Swords shows a figure lying prone, ten swords stabbed right into their exposed back. It is not a pretty sight and doesn't look like a fun place to be in at all. The figure is prone on a beach, next to a body of water, suggesting that they were somewhere comfortable, and this attack may well have come as a bit of a surprise.

The Ten of Swords is a tough hang. It's a card that reflects a deep sense of betrayal, loss, or emotional pain. When this card comes up, it's likely that something in your life has come to a sharp, sudden, and painful ending. This is the card that comes up when you get fired out of nowhere or a friend betrays your trust. It's a hard place to be, but it does mean that you're closing a chapter so a new one can begin.

The Ten of Swords can also come up when you're still working through something that made you feel this way long ago. It may be that a deep wound from the past has begun hurting you again, either because a current situation brought it up or just because it's an unhealed wound that's now asking to be tended.

Journal Questions for the Ten of Swords

• What does this card bring up? Does the image remind you of a current situation or one from your past?

• If you're walking through the Ten of Swords right now, be gentle with yourself. Take a moment to list some small things you can do to tend to your injuries, emotions, or otherwise.

• Consider the last time you went through that Ten of Swords feeling, that utter sense of loss and a sudden end. What did you do to get through it? How do you feel about the situation now after looking back? Did the ending make way for a new beginning?

• What would it look like to be reborn after this Ten of Swords moment? With this ending, what new things can you let into your life, when you're ready?

• If you're feeling betrayed right now, consider whether the relationship can or should be salvaged. If it can, spend some time working through what you'd like to see happen next in this relationship. If it can't, take some time to say goodbye, honoring what that person was to you and letting them go.

Court Cards and the Swords

With the ten-card journey complete, we've reached the Court Cards in the suit of Wands. Here, we see different reflections of creativity and creation as we walk through the phases of Page, Knight, Queen, and King. Each member of the court of Wands has a different lesson to share and a different aspect of the wand's fiery energy for us.

CHAPTER 65

Get Curious with the
Page of Swords

Page of Swords

The Page of Swords is curiosity embodied. It's a card full of energy and excitement about learning new things and taking in new surroundings. This is the card you might pull at the start of a trip to a new place, the beginning of a new educational program, or when you're just starting to get into a new hobby and can't get enough of it. For me, this card embodies how I fell headfirst into learning to play *Dungeons & Dragons* a few years ago. It was new, it was exciting, and it was all I wanted to talk and learn about. I needed to know all the things, all at once. That's the Page of Swords for you.

In the traditional Rider-Waite depiction, the Page of Swords stands at the edge of a mountain. He's holding a sword aloft with both hands, ready to charge forward... and yet, he is totally looking the other way because he doesn't want to miss what's going on over there, either. The clouds in the background are puffy and billowing, making interesting shapes that I'm sure our Page will want to check out, too. There's a river below and a tree in the background, representing the fertile nature of the Page's enthusiasm for learning. He's young, he's eager, and he wants to get this journey started. He doesn't want to miss a thing.

When the Page of Swords comes up, it's time to get curious. Maybe you already are, and this card reflects that you've found something to be enthusiastically interested in. Or maybe you're not, and it's time to tap into that curious mind and open up to what's going on around you. You just might encounter a new idea or way of doing things that will change your life.

Journal Questions for the Page of Swords

• Where do you see yourself in the images of this card? Do you have your head in the clouds like the Page? Are you the steady tree in the background, rooted in your ways? Take some time to consider which images resonate, and why.

• What sets your soul on fire? When was the last time you were this eager to learn something new, to dive headfirst into a project or hobby?

• How do you learn? Whether you're embarking on something new right now or seeking out that beginner's enthusiasm, consider how you best absorb new information. Should you listen to a podcast about the topic you're curious about? Read a book? Attend a course?

• The Page is depicted on the edge of something. What might be on your horizon that is just about to come into view? Can you foresee something new that will spark your curiosity? Can you find something to chase?

• Where in your life could you use a little bit of a refresh? Consider your relationships, patterns, and habits. Could you bring some fresh energy to any of these areas of your life right now?

CHAPTER 66

Knight of Swords

Where the Page is excited and eager to learn, the Knight is ready to *do the thing*, full speed ahead. He's made his decision, and he's probably made it quickly, so now he's charging in to take action, like right now. This is a card that's all about forward momentum and making things happen.

In the Rider-Waite depiction, the Knight of Swords is clearly charging into battle full speed ahead. He's fully armored, his cape blowing in the wind, kicked up by his horse. And that horse is booking it, racing ahead full throttle while his rider holds a sword in the air. You can practically hear him shouting "Charge!" Even the trees in the background are bent back as if, by the wind, the sheer movement in this card embraces even them.

When the Knight of Swords comes up, it's time to put your

thoughts into action. You've been thinking about something for a while, and the thinking time is over. Now it's time to make a decision and act on it, move forward, and get something done. This is a card for rolling up your sleeves and starting that project, that hobby, that thing you've been thinking about doing for a while. The Knight says the time is now now now, so let's go.

Journal Questions for the Knight of Swords

• What about this image draws your attention, and what message might that aspect of the card have for you at this moment?

• How often do you embody the Knight of Swords energy? In other words, are you someone who easily leaps into action? Or, do you tend to think things over and consider your options time and time again before slowly dipping a toe in? How has that served you?

• Is there something in your life that needs a bit of forward momentum right now? A decision you've made, but haven't acted on?

• If you've made the decision, what are you waiting for? Consider whether you have what you need to get started. If so, what's holding you back? If not, how can you get what you need to start this journey?

• Consider the trees in the background. Have you ever felt swept up by life, as if everything was moving around you and you were just caught in the wind? Maybe you feel like that now. What can you do to take back some ownership of your progress through life?

CHAPTER 67

Nurture Your Capabilities with the
Queen of Wands

Queen of Swords

The Queen of Swords is a firm, commanding presence when compared with some of our other Queen cards in the Tarot. Where so many of the Queens embody the softer sides of their suits, the Queen of Swords is comfortable and confident being in charge. This is a card about setting clear boundaries and expectations, about making your needs known and sticking to them. The Queen of Swords takes no nonsense, and she can be a bit direct at times, but sometimes, direct is what you need. As a people-pleaser, this card has haunted me in different periods of my life when I was doing far too much accommodating and not nearly enough enforcement of my own needs and boundaries.

In the Rider-Waite depiction, the Queen of Wands sits on her throne, shown from the side. She holds her sword upright, pointed towards the sky in a firm declaration of position. Her other hand reaches forward as if she is calmly speaking her piece about how things ought to be before hearing her subjects' side. Her throne depicts an angelic cherub on the side as well as a butterfly. They are little reminders that while the Queen stands firm in her convictions and sets boundaries, it doesn't mean she is uncaring or lacking the emotional intelligence of other Queens. She's just sure of where she stands and wants everyone else to know it, too.

The Queen of Swords comes up when you need to sort your boundaries. She's not going to let anyone take advantage of her and serves as a reminder that you shouldn't, either. Now is the time to speak your thoughts into reality and let people know what you're thinking. You can do it with tact and compassion, but it needs to be done. People can't respect the boundaries you never set, after all, so it's high time you set some.

Journal Questions for the Queen of Swords

• With this card, there's plenty to look at. Where is your attention drawn, and why do you think that is?

• This Queen knows where she stands. Do you? Consider the boundaries you've set in your life. What needs do they serve, and how well have you upheld them?

• Are there places in life where you need to speak your mind, but haven't? Take some time to note any situations where you've been holding back, and why that might be. Is it safe for you to express your thoughts and needs in this situation? If so, make a plan to do so. If not, consider what it would take for you to be able to express yourself freely here.

• What is your typical communication style? Are you able to be direct with your thoughts and feelings, or do you tend to hedge and try to be gentle when expressing what you think? How has this served you?

• What is your relationship to independence? Are you someone who prefers to be alone, to do things your own way in your own time? Or do you rely on others? How do you feel about this?

CHAPTER 68

Embrace What You Know with
the King of Swords

King of Swords

Ah, the King of Swords. A figure who is sure of himself, his intellect, and what he knows to be true. This is a King who has thought things through and knows what's best, and he is perfectly capable of exercising his authority to make it so. This card reflects those moments when you're using your head over your heart, making the right decision based on logic and facts. Sometimes, this is what life calls for, and the King of Swords is here to remind us to use our minds and think things through.

The King of Swords shows a king sitting on his throne, facing you head-on. He sits tall, yes, but almost casually so. His sword is held upright, but it tilts a bit to the left. He is so sure of his rightness and his authority that he doesn't need to put on any airs about it. This King takes up space and stands firm in his ground because he's right, not because he's putting on a show. His throne, like the Queen of Swords, shows butterflies and moons as a reminder that having authority and being creative and generous aren't mutually exclusive. You can be both. The fertile grounds around him show that the kingdom is doing well under his rule, and that he's right to think he's, well, right.

When the King of Swords comes up, it's time to trust what you know. If you've thought something through and really used your logical thinking skills to arrive at a conclusion, then you're probably spot on. If you did the math and you just can't take that job your heart wants because it'll never pay the bills, sadly, you're probably right about that and this is a situation where you need to follow your mind, not your feelings. If you're still trying to make a decision and you see this King, it's time for a pro and con list. Apply some hard logic to the choice you haven't been able to make with your gut.

Journal Questions for the King of Swords

• What draws your attention with this card? What images or aspects resonate with you at this time, and why might that be?

• What is your relationship to trusting your own decisions? Are you someone who can come to a conclusion and follow through, or is your head always at war with your heart? How has this worked out for you in the past?

• Have you made a choice using your reasoning? Now is the time to follow through. Write down what you decided, how you got there, and where you need to go from here.

• Still working something through? Make a pro and con list. Write your way through every angle of this situation and use the facts to make your decision.

• It may be that this card came up because you need to exercise your authority with a decision right now. Is this something you can do easily, or do you shy away from being the one in charge? How might you be able to step into your power and follow through on what you know to be true, even if it's not a comfortable and natural thing for you to do?

CHAPTER 69

Pentacles, or the Coins, are sometimes known and often associated with money and finances. They are, however, also representatives of other aspects of our material lives: the here and now, and the grounded reality of our physical realm. The Pentacles align with the element of Earth, meaning they're the solid foundation upon which we build our lives. They might mean money, yes, but they might also mean stability, the home and hearth, and other aspects which are a grounding presence and necessity for life. When the Pentacles come up, it's a reminder that we can't only tend to our mental and spiritual selves 24/7. Our physical bodies and surroundings need some love and attention, too.

CHAPTER 70

Ace of Pentacles

The Ace of Pentacles, like most of our Aces, is about a fresh start, a new beginning. Because this suit is about the material realm and finances, this card often reflects a new financial opportunity or some kind of growth in your career. It can also signify a time that's ripe for manifesting abundance, in whatever way you seek it—an abundance of money, sure, or an abundance of new experiences, relationships, etc. This card is about setting the foundation for plenty in the future.

In its Rider-Waite rendition, the Ace of Pentacles shows a hand extended from a fluffy cloud, holding a single coin aloft. In the background, we see a lush garden full of flowers, showing a great deal of growth and vibrancy. The hand is holding the first coin of many, it seems, a building block towards greater stability and wealth. If a journey begins with a single step, this path towards wealth begins with a single coin.

The Ace of Pentacles can be quite a literal card, showing up when you're on the brink of a new job offer or an unexpected infusion of cash. Or it may be a smaller opportunity, like the chance to expand your network or save a bit more than usual this month. This card can also be a sign that you need to adjust your money mindset away from a sense of scarcity towards one drawing money towards you (easier said than done, I know). When the Ace of Pentacles comes up, it's time to take a look at what you've got in terms of resources and see whether you can make any changes or embrace any opportunities that have come your way.

Journal Questions for the Ace of Pentacles

• What do you see when you look at your version of this card? What speaks to you or what do you find yourself resisting about the imagery?

• If the mysterious hand emerging from this cloud could hand you any opportunity, what would it be? What is it that you want to bring into your life at this moment?

• Consider your relationship to abundance. Do you tend to feel like you never have enough? Or is money not a concern for you? What about your past and your present have created that story for you, and how is it serving you?

• Look around you. Are there any opportunities to enrich your life that you haven't noticed or been open to?

• Since this is the card of manifestation, let's do a little bit of manifesting. Write down what you want to call into your life. Be specific and clear. Are you seeking a new job or just a bit more recognition of the one you have? Perhaps you have financial abundance, but you would love to upgrade your home space or your love life. Jot down what you want to manifest as if you already have it.

CHAPTER 71

Two of Pentacles

The Two of Pentacles is a card near and dear to my heart as someone with a history of juggling multiple part-time and freelance gigs. This card is all about balancing your priorities and responsibilities; it's about trying to keep all the plates spinning so you can meet your goals and needs. It's the card I pulled *all the time* in grad school when I was trying to manage coursework and two part-time jobs. The Two of Pentacles reminds us we can't always do it all, all the time. We need to set priorities and keep things in balance by knowing what is most essential and what can wait until tomorrow.

In Two of Pentacles, we see a figure that looks a bit like a court jester in his jaunty cap. He's holding two pentacles, one slightly higher than the other. Around them is a ribbon that forms itself into the infinity sign. Right now, he's got things under control, in balance. Yet we can see that one pentacle is above the other, suggesting it may have a higher priority right now. In the background, we see an ocean full of big waves, with two boats on either side of our juggling figure. One is smaller, yet finds itself in calmer seas, while the other is larger and in rougher waters. Here again, the idea that balance doesn't always mean treating everything equally, but rather adjusting the energy put in based on what is most important.

Journal Questions for the Two of Pentacles

• What stands out to you as you look at this card? What images draw your attention, and what might they have to say?

• Are you juggling a lot of responsibilities right now? Chances are if you've pulled this card, the answer is yes. Write out a list of all your to-dos and obligations. Then, spend some time ranking them in terms of importance. What is essential, and what *feels* important but could really be put off a bit longer if necessary?

• What does balance look like for you? Consider what is important to you, what nourishes you, and what you'd rather not have to do if you had your choice. Now, what can you do to make your life look a little bit more like this idea of balance?

• It's tempting to juggle all the coins on our own, but sometimes prioritizing is about delegation, as well. Look at your list of responsibilities again. Can you delegate or ask for help with any of this?

• What is your relationship to being busy? Do you enjoy having a lot of different plates spinning, or do you prefer to focus in on one or two tasks? How does your current life relate to your preferences in this area?

CHAPTER 72

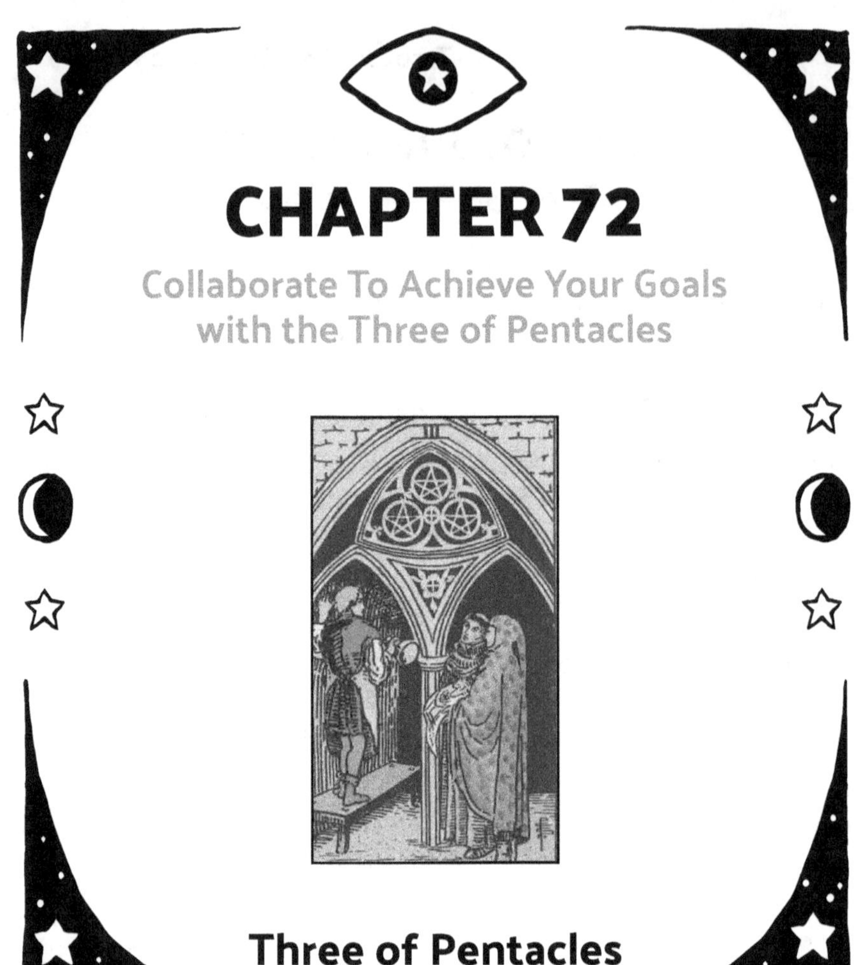

Three of Pentacles

If the Two of Pentacles is about trying to balance things on your own, the Three of Pentacles is a welcome reminder about the importance and value of teamwork. This card is all about collaboration, working together for a common goal or purpose. This often relates to the workplace, but it doesn't always. We can collaborate on volunteer projects, on artwork, on all manner of different things outside of work, as well. When the Three of Pentacles comes up, though, it's likely time to lean into working together and stop shouldering everything on your own.

In the Rider-Waite depiction, the Three of Pentacles shows three figures inside a building that looks a good bit like a place of worship. One figure stands on a bench, holding a tool. They seem to be working on building something. Two other figures stand nearby, holding out a piece of cloth. They are supervising, it seems, but also standing by to provide aid if needed. Above them is a stained-glass mural depicting three pentacles, showing what has already been created through their collective effort.

This card is about building something with other people. It's a reminder that no matter how self-sufficient you are, we all need a bit of help every now and again. When the Three of Pentacles comes up, take some time to look around you and see where you can be a bit more collaborative, lean into teamwork, or ask for help.

Journal Questions for the Three of Pentacles

• Take a look at this card and reflect on its images. What symbols or figures draw your attention? Do you relate to any of them? Why might that be?

• What is your relationship to teamwork? Do you tend to be a "do it yourself" type, or is it relatively easy for you to ask for help when you need it? Consider how this has worked out for you in the past.

• Do you have a big project or goal right now? Are you going it alone, or working with others? If you're riding solo, consider who you might be able to collaborate with. If you are working as a team, are there more ways you can effectively work together?

• When you're working as a team, which role do you tend to take on? Are you a leader or a follower? Do you shoulder more of the work than others in the team? Take some time to reflect on your past and present collaborative experiences and whether they are what you'd like them to be.

• Maybe you prefer to do things on your own, and you aren't looking to work with other people. If so, perhaps this card is an invitation to call on spiritual allies. If you're looking for help on a project that's more of the spiritual/higher power variety, take some time to jot down what kind of support you're looking for and then do some research into what plant allies, crystals, or other energies might be able to form your "team" at this moment.

CHAPTER 73

Four of Pentacles

The Four of Pentacles is a complicated card with a multifaceted meaning. It's about saving money or hoarding resources, something that can be a valuable and important thing to do. However, it's also about scarcity and greed, suggesting that there's such a thing as clinging *too* tightly to our material possessions. The Four of Wands is about saving and managing our resources, but not to such an extent that we forget to be generous with ourselves and others when the circumstances call for it.

The typical image for the Four of Pentacles shows a figure sitting outside of a town, clutching a coin to their chest for dear life. Another coin sits atop their head, suggesting a preoccupation with money and material things. Under each foot there is yet another pentacle, both showing that finances can form a solid foundation but also that our figure is using every bit of their body to hang on to the four coins they've got. They're not going to be able to do much else with themselves while they're holding this pose by hanging on to their money.

When the Four of Pentacles shows up for you, it's possible you're in a period where it feels like you're scrimping and saving just to make ends meet. Perhaps you had a few unexpected expenses that left you behind on bills, or perhaps you've been living paycheck-to-paycheck for a while and still not making much headway. Whatever the situation, it's likely that money and material stability are taking up a lot of your energy right now, quite possibly for good reason. This card is a reminder that while we do need a certain level of resources to exist in this world, we also have to attend to our other needs in order to live full lives. Things might be scant right now, and saving might be a worthwhile goal, but don't get so caught up in clutching coins that you forget to live.

Journal Questions for the
Four of Pentacles

• How do you relate to the imagery on this card? Does the figure feel familiar, or are you maybe more drawn to the background or one of the coins they're holding?

• Reflect on your money story for a moment. Are you a saver or a spender? Why might that be?

• What is the reality of your material situation right now? If you're in a period of saving, saving, saving, is that truly necessary, or is it coming from a place of past scarcity and fear? If it is necessary, are there ways you can bring some cost-free joy into your life to take your mind off the challenges of your material situation, if only for a little while?

• What *is* stable in your life right now? Do you have steady relationships, a place to live, and a consistent job? Consider what those coins your feet are resting on might be and take a moment to express gratitude for what you *do* have.

• If you're in a place where money or other resources are abundant for you, the Four of Pentacles may well be a reminder not to hoard your wealth. How can you share what you have and give back to those who have less?

CHAPTER 74

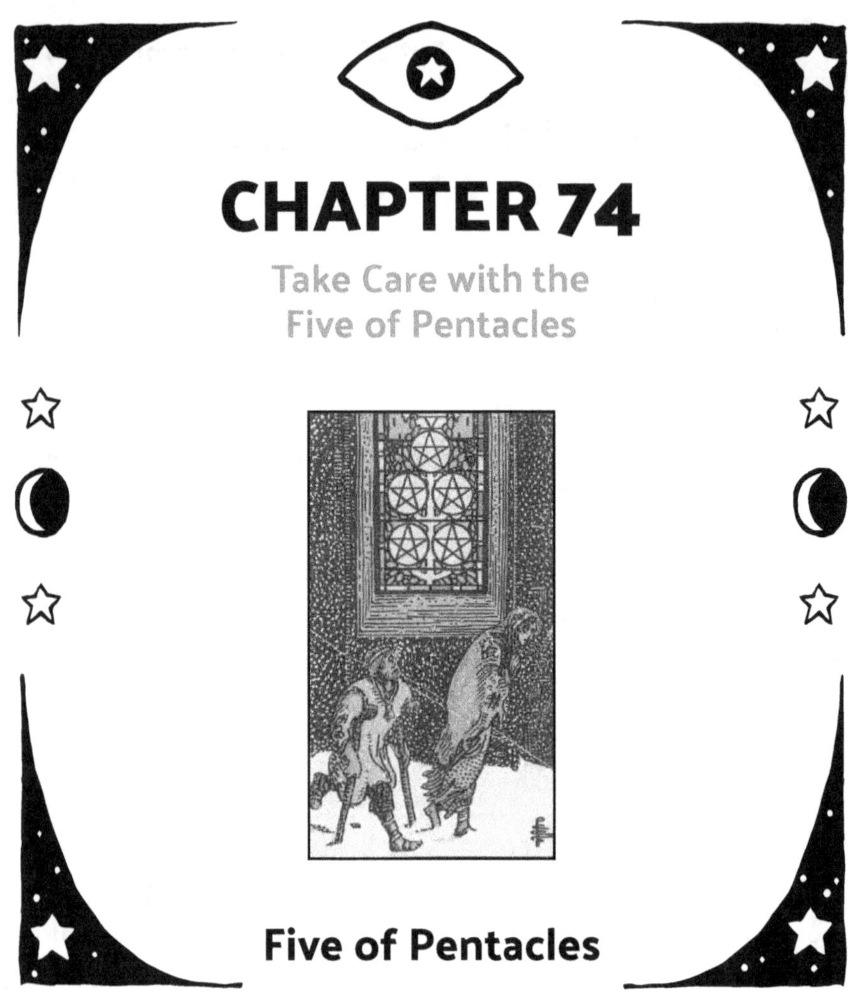

Five of Pentacles

The Five of Pentacles is another one of those cards that's a bit hard not to greet with a wince. It's a card suggesting lack, poverty, or recent injury or loss. It's a down on your luck, struggling to get back on track, a card that can be a difficult one to navigate. However, there's also a more uplifting message hidden in this relatively sad card—help and support might be closer than we think if we only open ourselves up to receiving it.

In the Rider-Waite version of the Five of Pentacles, we see two figures who are quite frankly going through it. In the front, a woman is hunched over, wrapped in a tattered shawl. She looks defeated, but she marches on anyway, determined to keep on trudging through the snow. Behind her is a smaller figure, perhaps a child, with bandages on their feet and head. He's walking with crutches but seems a bit more full of energy than the foremost figure. Both of them are clearly struggling and trying to keep going on their own. In the background, we see an inviting stained-glass window, a sanctuary that might offer help and support if only the two of them looked in that direction instead of so steadfastly forward.

When you pull the Five of Pentacles, you may well have suffered a recent loss or setback. This is the "just lost your job" card, the unexpected expenses you weren't prepared for card, the card that comes up when the blows just keep coming. In part, it's a reminder that we all have these difficult experiences sometimes—they're just a part of life. And yes, sometimes we have to keep on pushing through the snow even when we're tired and cold. However, the key message in this card isn't just an affirmation that times really are tough. It's that sometimes, times are partly tough because we aren't letting ourselves see the ways in which we could accept help. If you're struggling, you may not have to do it alone. Consider where you might turn to for a bit of temporary help or support as you navigate this tough time. One day, maybe, you'll be able to pay it back, but right now that's not what matters. Getting back on your feet is what matters.

Journal Questions for the
Five of Pentacles

• Where in this card do you see yourself right now? Are you the downtrodden woman, plodding forward? The youth on crutches, trying to bring their full energy to the situation even though they're bruised and broken? Or does something else in the card speak to you right now?

• Are you navigating a difficult situation right now? Take some time to honor where you are and grieve the recent loss or challenges. Just sit with your feelings and write them down. Don't try to fix it right now. Just let it be, so you can begin to process it.

• Consider past situations that gave you the Five of Pentacles feeling if you can. Presumably, you got through those hard times. How did you get to the other side? Who or what helped back then? Do you have access to those things now?

• Where might you be able to seek help and support for whatever is challenging you at this moment? If you're behind on bills, is there an aid program to which you can apply? If you lost a job, can you file unemployment or lean on your network to help you find a new gig? Spend some time exploring your options for aid, rather than just continuing to push forward on your own.

• Perhaps you're not struggling so much in this very moment but know someone who is. Have you asked them how and if you can help? Can you give back your time in another way, through volunteering or donations to a cause?

CHAPTER 75

Give Freely When You Can with the Six of Pentacles

Six of Pentacles

The Six of Pentacles is a foil to the Five in so many ways. Where the Five reflects scarcity, the Six of Pentacles is about giving back. This card is a reminder to give what you can and when you can to those who are less fortunate than you. Whatever you have in abundance (time, resources, money, knowledge) should be shared with those who have less. In so many ways this card is about charity and generosity for its own sake, but there's also a subtle reminder to treat others as you'd want to be treated, too. You may be able to give now, but one day you might be the one needing assistance, so don't be stingy with what you have lest others be stingy with you.

In the Rider-Waite illustrations, the Six of Pentacles feature a figure in very fine, lavish robes. In one hand, they hold a balanced scale, a reminder that what goes up must come down, and that often includes our own stability and good fortune. The figure has an abundance of wealth now, as illustrated by the coins that flow freely from their hand into the hands of the beggar beside them. However, the scale is a reminder that things may not be this way forever, and that the figure who is giving of their wealth now might be asking for help in the future—or indeed, perhaps they already have. The two figures on the ground are shrouded in thick, tattered robes, suggesting their status as impoverished people seeking help and support. Their pose is one of gratitude and awe at the figure who bestows generosity upon them. This can suggest that they don't see this sort of kindness often, or that they are simply in awe of the fortunes of this figure.

When the Six of Pentacles comes up, it's an invitation to consider how you can give to those around you. Perhaps that is in the form of financial support to a cause, but maybe it's a more subtle generosity. Perhaps you can lend some extra time to volunteer, or maybe you have some knowledge you can share with someone who needs it. The Six of Pentacles asks you to consider where your wealth in life lies and how you can spread it around a bit.

Journal Questions for the Six of Pentacles

• Where do you see yourself in this card at the current moment? Are you the figure of abundance and generosity, or are you the one asking for help?

• Where does your abundance lie? Consider the resources available to you. What do you have plenty of in your life? Friendship? Love? A roof over your head?

• How can you give back? Consider the ways you can bring some positivity into the world, even if it isn't through a traditional donation or volunteer position.

• When have you needed support in your life, and where has it come from? Consider what you've needed in difficult times and whether those needs were met.

• What is your relationship to giving and receiving help? Are you easily able to offer support to others when you sense they need it, or is this difficult for you? Are you able to accept help, or does your pride or fear of being a burden get in the way? How has this served you in the past?

CHAPTER 76

Sow What You Hope to Reap with
the Seven of Pentacles

Seven of Pentacles

You know the expression "reap what you sow?" Well, before you can harvest anything, you've got to plant it first. The Seven of Pentacles is a card that suggests now is the time to lay the foundation for what you want your life to be in the future. It's time to plan and take action to set your future self up for success. If you're a farmer like my husband, this can be taken pretty literally—plant those seeds in order to have a harvest when the farmer's market comes around. But for most of us, the planting is more metaphorical. If you want a new job, you've got to start the search. If you're hoping to find a loving relationship, you need to put yourself out there to meet someone. Whatever it is you're seeking, you've got to put in the work and plan to make it happen.

The Seven of Pentacles shows a figure leaning on a staff,

looking at a plant lush with coins. It's clear from how he rests on his staff that he's put in some work to make this happen, and now he's enjoying the sight of the coins he planted growing and approaching harvest time. The figure is a bit on the exhausted side, suggesting just how much effort it took to get this bountiful yield.

The message of this card is a straightforward one. When it comes up for you, it's time to plant those metaphorical seeds. Take some time to consider what you want to blossom into your life, and what steps you need to take now to set yourself up for that future bounty. It's a hard work card and a put your ideas into action kind of card, but it suggests that you'll see some benefit if you put in the work.

Journal Questions for the Seven of Pentacles

• What images draw your attention in this card? Do you find yourself drawn to the tired, hardworking figure? Or perhaps the harvest, the plant ripe with coins for the taking? Why might this be?

• What is it that you want to harvest in the future? Take some time to imagine life in one year, five years, however far out you feel called to plan. What would it look like if you achieved your goals?

• What should you plant now to ensure this harvest? In other words, what steps do you need to take here and now to prepare for this future version of your life?

• How do you approach hard work? What is your strategy for getting things done, for holding yourself accountable when things are difficult? Has this worked well in the past, or is it time to try a new approach?

• What is your relationship to rest? The figure in this card is exhausted from how hard he's worked, and he's going to need a break before he harvests all this bounty, or he may well burn-out. How can you effectively take breaks while still accomplishing your necessary tasks?

CHAPTER 77

Put in the Work with the Eight of Pentacles

Eight of Pentacles

The Eight of Pentacles is all about putting in the work. Planning and dreaming and manifesting are all well and good, but nothing comes into being without some effort. This card is all about being productive, making things, and checking off those to-do list items one by one. Sometimes this is because you've just got a long list of things to do, and other times it suggests a period of repeating the same task or tasks so you can learn to do it more effectively. Regardless, there's also a sense of pride in what you create: the solid satisfaction of a job well done.

In the Rider-Waite deck, the Eight of Pentacles shows a figure straddling their workbench. They're hammering away at a pentacle, with a line of completed ones already hung up beside them. A few more lie on the ground, ready to be worked on as well. This is someone who is dedicated, attentive, and get things done. We also see that they've come a long way and created a lot, but that they're still driving ahead to keep on working. Each pentacle is well made and symmetrical, suggesting that they're not just doing the work, but doing *good* work as well. These creations are something to be proud of and have likely taken years of hard work to learn to make so well.

When you pull the Eight of Pentacles, you're likely in a season where work and accomplishments take center stage. Perhaps you're prioritizing your career right now or working on a big creative project that takes a lot of dedication to see through. Maybe you've just changed career paths or started a new education program, something that will take a bit of repetition and hard work to master. Wherever you're at, when the Eight of Pentacles comes calling, it's time to focus in and do the work to hone your skills, complete the thing, and get to the next level of mastery.

Journal Questions for the Eight of Pentacles

• Looking at your version of this card, what stands out to you? Why might that be?

• What kind of work puts you in the "flow state" that we see on this card? In other words, when do you feel in the groove and able to keep working at something because it suits your skills or your interests?

• Is there something you're just starting to learn, that might require a good deal of repetition before you get good? What made you take on that new skill or role? Jot down why it's important to you, so you can reflect on this why when the work gets tough.

• What is your relationship to work right now? What does it mean to you to be productive, to get work done? Are you satisfied with your work or seeking a change?

• When is the last time you truly mastered something? When did you practiced a skill until you did it well? How did that feel?

CHAPTER 78

Enjoy What You Have with the Nine of Pentacles

Nine of Pentacles

If the lifestyle influencers of today had a Tarot card mascot, it'd be the Nine of Pentacles. This card is all about appreciating and enjoying what you've managed to build in your life. And with all the hard work and toil that precedes it in the Pentacles suit, is it any wonder the Nine is ready to sit back and enjoy the fruits of the labor? When I think of this card, I think of how I felt shortly after landing my first full-time, salaried position. After years of scraping by to make rent by cobbling together the profits from various part-time roles, sitting in one place and earning a steady paycheck for the first time felt *amazing*. I knew this wasn't my forever job, but in that moment, all I wanted to do was appreciate that I could afford to treat myself a bit. I wanted to buy new clothes, enjoy a few more meals out, and just generally bask in what my success (however temporary) had provided for me. That, in a nutshell, is your Nine of Pentacles energy.

Rider-Waite is a bit too old-school for Instagram influencer imagery, so it draws its inspiration from the nobility of old. In this image, we see a woman wearing a flowing robe and an elaborate headdress. She's walking through a lush garden ripe with grapes and coins. On her outstretched hand a hooded falcon perches, a symbol of nobility if I ever saw one. Falconry was a hobby for the upper class, and this woman is enjoying it as a simple pastime while she strolls through her lush and abundant gardens. Everything about her speaks of repose and ease, to enjoying what surrounds her to the very fullest.

When the Nine of Pentacles comes up, it is time to treat yourself. This might look different depending on what your abundance looks like these days, but you can get creative here. You've worked hard, and you deserve to spend at least a few moments enjoying what that hard labor has won for you. While the Nine of Pentacles itself gives off lush and relaxed vibes, it is also about the self-sufficient, hard-working attitude that brought you here. Pat yourself on the back and honor how far you've come, even if that looks like one 15-minute coffee break rather than a weekend away at the spa. Chances are if you're seeing this card, you've earned it.

Journal Questions for the
Nine of Pentacles

• Sit with the imagery of this card in whichever deck you're working with. What do you feel drawn to and why might that be?

• What does luxury mean to you? What are the little treats you enjoy giving to yourself when you're able to? Can you afford to have one of them right now?

• Consider what independence and self-sufficiency mean to you. Are you someone who enjoys providing for yourself, or are you part of a couple or relationship where both parties contribute equally? How does this setup serve you?

• Make a "treat yourself" list. Even if you don't think you have the time, money, and energy for these things right now, just take some time to write down all the ways you'd enjoy the fruits of your labor if you could. The next time you need a little self-care, turn back to this list and see if you can give yourself anything on it.

• Do you feel abundant right now? Consider what you have in excess in your life, what you have enough of, and anywhere that there may be a lack. What would it take for you to feel like you have enough to let yourself rest?

CHAPTER 79

Appreciate What You've Built with the Ten of Pentacles

Ten of Pentacles

The Ten of Pentacles invites us to celebrate how far we've come in our quest to build stability in our material world. This card suggests a place of financial security, of being able to build a life and a family because of the solid foundation you've created. This is a long-term success, setting up generational wealth kind of card, which can be tricky for those of us who have more of a foundation of debt than the kind of money that buys houses in which to raise kids and dogs. Even so, the message of this card invites us to appreciate what we *have* built and what success looks like for us. Maybe you're not rolling in cash, but you're chasing a dream career. Perhaps you're saddled with student loans and are likely to rent for the foreseeable future, but your life is rich with loving relationships. The Ten of Pentacles is success and stability, but it looks different depending on who we are.

In the Rider-Waite rendition, the Ten of Pentacles shows a wizened old figure kneeling down to pet one of two dogs in the scene. He is looking out over a young man and woman, who have a small child in tow. We get the sense that perhaps this is grandpa enjoying a look at the next generation his hard work and wealth have helped to support. The image gives off the sense of a big, happy family with enough to go around that they have not one, but *two* pets to share their abundance with. In the background, we see a wall, suggesting that they are well-off enough to have their own private, guarded space in which to thrive as a unit.

When this card comes up, it's often an omen of success to come. It's a pat on the back that says you're building something worthwhile here, or even that you've already built it. The Ten of Pentacles invites us to consider what we've built already, the foundation we've created. You may not be trying to start a family, but chances are you've done something to advance towards the vision of a happy, healthy life that you will be able to look back on one day with the satisfaction of this old man appreciating his family line. Sometimes, this card can also be about exploring or considering our legacy, what we hope to leave behind to future generations, as well.

Journal Questions for the Ten of Pentacles

• So many people and living beings to look at in this card! Take some time with this card and consider which figure best fits where you see yourself in your journey. Are you the young couple just starting to build a life, or the old man looking on at the next generation? Perhaps you're the child, barely getting started, or even the dog, just enjoying life without a big future plan.

• What would you like to see when you look back on your legacy? If you're the old man looking fondly at what you've built, what is it that you hope to see? Do you want to leave behind a big, happy family? A series of artworks in a museum? A published memoir?

• This is a tough one, but the card kind of demands we think about it. What do financial stability and wealth mean to you? What would it take for you to feel secure in your finances? How can you move in that direction if you aren't already?

• What is your money story? In other words, how do you feel when you think about the idea of amassing wealth? Does it feel impossible, like a distant dream meant only for other people? Have you come from a place of scarcity that seems ever-present? Or have you led a life where you can generally trust that you'll have what you need?

• What does family mean to you? This card's traditional image invites us to view the family structure as a success, but that doesn't fit all of us. What was family like for you growing up? What does family mean to you now?

Court Cards and the Pentacles

For the Pentacles, our court cards are all about ways of approaching material wealth and stability. They're looking at how to be or become more grounded, more practical, really channeling that Earth energy through the spirit of our Page, Knight, Queen, and King. If you've got (or you are) that reliable friend who's always has a first-aid kit on hand, that's the energy we're getting from this court.

CHAPTER 80

Page of Pentacles

I love a Page of Pentacles moment. This youthful energy is all about the start of a new opportunity, often a financial one. It's that shiny first job offer, or the one you've been waiting for. It's learning something new to get ready to start off on a new and different career path. It's putting your energy into dreaming up what you want your financial life to look like, manifesting something new that will serve you better. This card, like all the Pages, is about the beginner's mindset or being a real and actual beginner, and often, it's in the realm of work or a career. If apprenticeships were still a common thing, this would be your apprenticeship card.

In the Rider-Waite illustration, the Page of Pentacles stands in a lush field full of possibility and potential. He is dressed snappily, as if trying to impress on their first day, and honestly, that's probably what they're up to. He is holding a giant coin aloft with both hands like he can't quite believe how precious this new opportunity is and doesn't want to drop it. His focus is on this new opportunity and all his energy is towards making it a reality.

I love to see the Page of Pentacles in a reading, particularly for someone who's been struggling with their career path or next steps when it comes to work. This card is so full of potential energy that it's hard not to congratulate whoever this card is speaking to. Even if it's not an actual job offer (though, it often can be), this card signifies an opportunity to start anew or learn something new. Maybe you want to stick with your current job, but you see an opportunity for advancement or a skills class you can take to brush up on the latest in the field. When this card comes up, look out for new opportunities in the realms of work and finance, because they may well be around. This can also signify growing knowledge and skills in a hobby or another area of life as well. So, if you're not in a career-forward place, this card may still have something to offer you.

Journal Questions for the Page of Swords

• What does the imagery of this card bring up for you? What comes to mind when you look at it? Are you drawn to specific elements?

• When was the last time you seized on a new opportunity? How did it go?

• Are you trying to bring something new into your life right now, whether it's work-related or another change you're hoping to see? Spend some time jotting down what it would look like to have that opportunity available to you.

• What are you learning right now? In what areas of your life are you growing or actively seeking new knowledge? If nothing comes to mind, where might you be able to grow and expand a bit?

• How do you approach new beginnings? Does change make you nervous, or do you welcome it? Take some time to consider how you can bring joy and excitement to starting something new, whether you're at that point right now or looking ahead to future new beginnings.

CHAPTER 81

Find a Productive Groove with the
Knight of Pentacles

Knight of Pentacles

Where the Page stares at his coin like it's something shiny and new, the Knight of Pentacles holds it aloft with confidence. The Knight knows what he's doing and has a routine for how he handles this whole coin-holding business. In its essence, the Knight of Pentacles is about finding and maintaining a routine; it's about getting into the groove for your working life or other areas where you're trying to build stability. He stands firm and confident in his day-to-day. This is you when you've been at the job long enough where you can do it in your sleep. It's a calm, confident routine you can keep at steadily while accomplishing all that you need to do.

The image of the Knight of Pentacles is interesting because this knight is *not* in motion like so many of the others. His horse has all four feet firmly planted on the ground, further illustrating the solid, stable energy of this card. The knight sits upright, leaning back a bit, and holding his single pentacle firmly aloft in a gloved hand. Everything about this card says, "I've got it all under control."

When you pull the Knight of Pentacles, one of two things is probably happening: you're in a space where you've settled into a solid routine, or you're in a space where you desperately need one. Either way, this card is about consistent, hard work, getting things done, and getting them done consistently. If you're in the groove, take time to note what helped you get there so you can find this space again when you need to. If you're not, take some time to plan out a bit more structure to support you.

Journal Questions for the Knight of Pentacles

• What does this card evoke for you? When you look at your version of the card, what draws your attention? How does it make you feel?

• Do you have a steady routine in your life? Are there certain habits or practices you turn to consistently? How is this working for you?

• If you don't have a routine, where in your life might you be able to build a bit more structure? Have you used a system to organize your time in the past? If not, maybe explore some options to manage your time.

• Do you feel grounded right now, or do you feel a bit adrift? If you are feeling grounded, what is contributing to that sense of stability? If you aren't, what might you need to help you feel a bit more solid?

• Do you relate to the Knight of Pentacles in his quiet confidence that he knows what he's doing? Or do you tend to second-guess yourself? Why might that be, and how is it working for you at this point in your life?

CHAPTER 82

Tend to What You Have with the
Queen of Pentacles

Queen of Pentacles

If there's one Queen who has the most Motherly energy, it's probably the Queen of Pentacles. This card is all about tending to and caring for the things that matter in your life, whether that's an actual child, a passion project, or a pet. This card brings all the nurturing energy, and often that includes support of a financial type as well. If you're working hard to give your kid (or your dog) a better life, that's your Queen of Pentacles energy.

The Queen of Pentacles depicts the Queen on her throne in a lush, lovely field. A vine grows around her, curling in a protective way as if to keep her sheltered and protected. Similarly, she leans over the pentacle in her lap, protecting and nurturing it as if it is something very dear to her—which, probably, it is. All of that caring seems to be doing some good if all the lush plant growth around is any indication. This is a stable image with a loving and tender energy to it.

When the Queen of Pentacles comes up, it's an invitation to tend to something. Tend to yourself, to your relationship, to your work, or to your hobbies. Whatever is near and dear to you could use some tender loving energy right now, and you're probably the one to bring it. On the other hand, this card may also come up when it's you who's seeking some of that archetypal mother energy, needing to be cared for or supported.

Journal Questions for the Queen of Pentacles

• What aspects of this card draw your attention, and what might they mean for you at this moment?

• What are you tending to in your life during this season? Are your energies going towards work, to the home, or to your relationships? Consider what you're nurturing right now.

• Consider your relationship to caretaking/mothering. Did you have a stable mother figure in your life, or did you have to mother yourself for all or most of your childhood? How has that impacted how you approach caring for yourself and others?

• What would it look like to take care of yourself the way you imagine your ideal mother figure would? How can you give some love and gentleness to your inner child in this moment, especially if you feel like you need it?

• Is there something in your life you'd like to spend more time tending to? Perhaps it's a long-forgotten hobby or a friendship that could use a bit more time and energy. Jot down a few areas where you might want to spend a bit more energy on in the future, and brainstorm how and when you might be able to do this.

CHAPTER 83

Settle Into Being in Charge with the King of Pentacles

King of Pentacles

The King of Pentacles is a man in charge, no doubt about it. This card brings in the energy of discipline, of wealth acquired through careful consideration and smart business decisions. This is a card that often reflects people in management positions and roles of leadership that allow them to make decisions and lead their company (or household) to a place of security and stability.

The image for the King of Pentacles shows a leader surrounded by abundance. He sits on an ornate throne, surrounded by lush plant life. His robes are full and he's sitting in a comfortable but confident sort of way, like he's in charge and he's at ease about it. In his left hand, he holds a pentacle firmly in his grasp, almost as if it's on display as a symbol of his wealth and power. One foot is visible under his robes, and it's firmly planted on a rock, showing that

Earth energy groundedness you might expect from the Pentacles. In his right hand, he's holding a scepter, a symbol of his power and authority. A castle looms off in the distance, signifying the kingdom over which this king confidently rules.

When you pull the King of Pentacles, it's time to channel those leadership skills and lean into your discipline. Whether you've been newly put in a leadership role at work or in life, or if it's just yourself you need to take charge of, this card calls you to channel your authority and take charge. This can be a tough card to connect with in all its security and status, but it's an energy we can all use from time to time.

Journal Questions for the King of Pentacles

• What about this card sticks out to you? Are you drawn to certain aspects of it, or do you feel pushed away by it? What message could that have for you?

• Do you consider yourself a leader? If you do, what skills help you step into that leadership role? If you don't, why not?

• What does "discipline" mean to you? Are you someone who sticks to a strict regime, or do you tend to have a bit of a looser structure with your life and schedule?

• If there's something you need to get done, it's time to be a bit of a manager to yourself. How can you bring structure into your life so you can accomplish your tasks?

• What does "security" mean to you? What would you need to have, be, or do to feel like this king sitting calmly upon his throne?

Conclusion: Where Do We Go from Here?

So, you've reached the end of the book. That, or you've flipped ahead to see what the conclusion is. Either way, welcome to the end, which is also the beginning. The joy of using Tarot for self-reflection is that the journey is never over, just like our ability to grow and change and adapt never really goes away, either.

I see this book a bit like the Wheel of Fortune, in that it just keeps on spinning. Even if you've journaled your way through every card in the Tarot, those are only the lessons it has to teach you right now, in *this* moment, in *this* season of your life. The beauty (and the tough part) of life is that we're never in the same exact place for very long. You can pick up the same card and look at the same five journal questions a year from now, and it might well mean something entirely different to you than it did back then. What that means is that you've got a wealth of self-growth and exploration at your disposal now that you've got the hang of journaling with the Tarot.

Any time you've got a decision to make or some thinking to do, any time you're looking to journal but aren't sure where to start, you can pull out your trusty Tarot deck or just use the images in this book, and you've got plenty to reflect upon and journal about. I hope that by the time you reach this point in the book, you've developed a relationship with the Tarot that can serve you well into the future. I know that my decks have seen me through some tough times and encouraged me to celebrate some great ones, and that I'm still finding new cards and new meanings even after studying them for all these years.

So where do you go from here, now that you've finished this book? You can keep on using it as a guide to help you connect with and work with the Tarot, if you like. These questions, these cards, these meanings, will always be here for you to turn to when you need a bit of guidance or a good dose of self-reflection. And really, just like we begin again when we reach The World in Tarot, you can start over at the Fool once again, ready to learn whatever the next cycle has to teach you.

ABOUT THE AUTHOR

Amanda Kay Oaks earned her MFA in Creative
Nonfiction from Chatham University and is a
certified Holistic Witch and Priestess. When she's not
contemplating her Tarot cards, Amanda writes about
books, video games, and pop culture on the internet.
She lives in a cabin in the woods near Pittsburgh, PA
with her husband and dog, Azula.